T0267244

Play Stories

play stories

Using Your Play Memories and Perspectives to Inform Teaching Practice

KATELYN CLARK

Redleaf Press®
www.redleafpress.org
800-423-8309

Published by Redleaf Press
10 Yorkton Court
St. Paul, MN 55117
www.redleafpress.org

© 2025 by Katelyn Clark

All rights reserved. Unless otherwise noted on a specific page, no portion of this publication may be reproduced or transmitted in any form or by any means, electronic or mechanical, including photocopying, recording, or capturing on any information storage and retrieval system, without permission in writing from the publisher, except by a reviewer, who may quote brief passages in a critical article or review to be printed in a magazine or newspaper, or electronically transmitted on radio, television, or the internet.

First edition 2024
Cover design by Erin Kirk
Cover illustration by Khwanchai/Adobe Stock
Interior design by Louise OFarrell
Interior illustrations by Hibrida13/iStock
Typeset in Chaparral Pro
Printed in the United States of America

31 30 29 28 27 26 25 24   1 2 3 4 5 6 7 8

Library of Congress Cataloging-in-Publication Data
Names: Clark, Katelyn, 1978– author.
Title: Play stories : using your play memories and perspectives to inform
   teaching practice / Katelyn Clark.
Description: First edition. | St. Paul, MN : Redleaf Press, 2025. |
   Includes bibliographical references and index. | Summary: "Play Stories
   invites early childhood educators to reflect deeply on their own
   childhood experiences and adult play and build their understanding of
   how their own identities shape their perspectives on children's play.
   Writing the stories of their own play provides a new platform for
   educators to understand their play pedagogy from a more holistic
   perspective and to identify where they really playfully shine in their
   classrooms, to become more invested in the play of their students"—
   Provided by publisher.
Identifiers: LCCN 2024026554 (print) | LCCN 2024026555 (ebook) | ISBN
   9781605548166 (paperback) | ISBN 9781605548173 (ebook)
Subjects: LCSH: Play. | Early childhood education. | Child development.
Classification: LCC LB1139.35.P55 C53 2025 (print) | LCC LB1139.35.P55
   (ebook) | DDC 372.13—dc23/eng/20240718
LC record available at https://lccn.loc.gov/2024026554
LC ebook record available at https://lccn.loc.gov/2024026555

Printed on acid-free paper

To Alice and Joe: my ultimate source for joyful play

Contents

Acknowledgments

I want to thank the four teachers who shared their play stories with me. Thank you for jumping in with both feet to engage with your cherished childhood memories. Your honesty, generosity, and playfulness were invigorating, and your stories are the heart of this work.

INTRODUCTION

We Teach What
We Are

PLAY HAS ALWAYS BEEN A SOURCE of joy and meaning in my life. My childhood was full of what I consider to be rich play experiences. Pretending. Becoming someone or something else. In the New England woods throughout the 1980s, my sister and I spent our free time creating long and elaborate storylines that would break only for the occasional meal or inevitable disagreement. We created imaginary characters: inventing and reinventing ourselves as horses galloping through the forest, concerned mothers taking care of our babies, or shopkeepers in our makeshift store. We filled our days engaging with the materials around us, pretending to be surgeons pulling rotting wood out of a tree stump or hairdressers chopping off all of Barbie's hair. We played until bedtime—sometimes past bedtime!—and I couldn't get out of bed fast enough in the morning to go wake up my sister and start playing again. I look back on this period of my childhood as valuable and magical.

These nostalgic feelings I hold for my own dramatic play experiences have shaped my career as an early childhood educator. My teaching philosophy reflected these sentiments around dramatic play, and I began to place significant value on it in the classroom in which I taught. In both formal and informal contexts, I would utilize dramatic play as a vehicle for learning, from themed props and costumes in the dress-up corner to dramatized storytelling at circle time. Play, but specifically dramatic play, was a hallmark of my curriculum development and teaching practice.

However, I began to notice that my colleagues and I did not share the same interests in play: one teacher prioritized movement and would break out her guitar for dancing at the drop of a hat, while another held a more observational, hands-off approach to play. I had assumed we had shared beliefs surrounding which play experiences were the most valuable and what constituted "good play," when, in actuality, these evaluations were very personal. These personal evaluations of play became more evident as I began to talk with teachers about their own experiences.

I am talking about childhood with my friend Karen, who is shocked that I have never played kick the can. "You don't know kick the can?" Karen spent her childhood in a small town in Maine and grew up playing outside in the street and in the woods. Karen and her siblings played outside until five, when they were called in for dinner, even on the coldest of Maine winter days. In our reminiscing about our own childhood play, she began to talk thoughtfully about how she sees children playing now. Throughout her twenty-three-year career as an educator in the New York City school system, Karen has identified strongly as someone who values not only play, but specifically outdoor play. As a classroom teacher, she would skip her own lunch period to make sure her students got outside every day, rain or shine—and her attitude toward and practice around play eventually spread to her coworkers. Later, as an administrator, Karen continued to proactively encourage these kinds of choices by mandating a similar kind of commitment to play with the staff at her school. She scolded an imaginary teacher, "No, I don't care if it's snowing outside, you go outside. I don't care if it's thirty degrees outside, you go outside and you play."

Karen's personal choice to prioritize the outdoors has shaped her identity as a practitioner who supports a specific type of play. Karen and I are different people: our understandings of play are specific to a very particular geographic, cultural, and social context, rather than a shared experience. We have different backgrounds and different priorities when it comes to the play of young children, but we both *have priorities*.

Play Stories: Using Your Play Memories and Perspectives to Inform Teaching Practice is inspired by the many conversations like this that I have had with fellow early childhood educators. Teachers' specific experiences of childhood play and their particular career trajectory may be unique, but the interconnectedness of personal play history and the choices surrounding play they make in practice are not. The resonance and relevance of an educator's history with play is a key piece in understanding play pedagogy. A teacher's play pedagogy is the practical expression of their personal and professional ideas about play in the early childhood classroom (Ryan and Northey-Berg 2014)—it is the lens through which teachers approach their own notions of the value attached to childhood play.

My position in the field is a result of a long journey that began with a love of teaching and dramatic arts. After completing my undergraduate degree in early childhood, I promptly moved to New York to pursue a career in the theater. I attended a theater arts program and hit the pavement chasing a dream. It was here where the interconnected relationship between play, drama, and early education began to take shape, as I worked with young children to pay the bills throughout my time as an actor. As this passion for education and drama grew, I found myself teaching full-time in a classroom and acting on the side! I was drawn to working within the overlap of my interests: theater, play, and young children. I went on to receive a master's degree in educational theater, followed by a doctoral degree in early childhood education, all with a research agenda focused on the play of young children and teachers' engagement with play.

This book is the culmination of a dissertation study I conducted in 2017 with four teachers (whose names have been changed) from a small lab school. The teachers took part in two play story interview sessions as well as one large focus group. In addition, I spent time observing each of the teachers at work in the classroom to gain a deeper understanding of who these individuals were both personally and professionally. The end result was four rich, varied stories about a lifetime with play that I will share with you here in chapters 4 through 7. They are shining examples of the power of creating a play story and will guide us in the development of our own play stories throughout this book.

This process, the act of creating and sharing play stories, brings to light a very specific, experience-based way of knowing about play. In the telling of our history with play, we engage with our interests, preferences, and skills: as players, and ultimately as facilitators of play. In taking part in this reflective practice, teachers awaken a sense of selfhood and identity around play that they carry with them into the classroom every day. This book explores the process of creating a play story as a way of understanding and reflecting on play pedagogy in a deep meaningful way, with its foundation in the notion that we *teach* what we *are*.

How to Use This Book

My hope is that while reading, you will be inspired to do some reflecting of your own on your personal play story. Throughout the book, you will find places to reflect on and write about what you are reading and to document some of your personal and professional impressions on play. If you find these reflections to be triggering or a source of stress in any way, please stop—this is not the reflective practice for you right now. If you are facilitating this work, please be aware that this work is not meant to be therapeutic; take stock of the emotional needs of the participants and allow space for other avenues of reflection. Play memories are not always pleasant and can be related to childhood trauma, so if you are in distress, please seek out the professional help you need to process these memories in a safe environment.

These writing prompts are meant to connect the reading to your own experiences and to possibly get a jump-start at developing your own play story. You can use a journal of your own or write in the spaces provided in the book. Later, in the appendix of this book, you will find a full play story interview protocol for you to use on your own or with a partner. Read, reflect, and enjoy!

REFLECT

Take a moment to free associate a bit around the word *play*. What other words come to mind when you think about play? What types of feelings arise when you think of play in the context of your own childhood? "Play is . . ."

CHAPTER 1

Teachers and Play

WALK INTO ANY early childhood classroom today and you will find evidence of play: from the shelves of blocks to the dress-up corner, play is considered a pillar of early childhood curriculum and a huge part of every young child's day. The role of play in the early childhood classroom has always been an evolving concept. Play has been a staple in early education, but its importance for young children's learning and development has fluctuated over the past fifty years.

Historically, play was considered to be a key piece of the early childhood curriculum and a crucial part of young children's learning and development. Policies like the No Child Left Behind Act (2001) and the more recent Race to the Top initiative (US Department of Education 2009) required states to adhere to early learning standards, which heightened pressure for academic performance in early education. As a result, play-based practices were in danger of being pushed entirely out of many early childhood classrooms (Hirsh-Pasek et al. 2009; Miller and Almon 2009). In a response to these academic pressures, both researchers and practitioners alike have sought to establish play as not a threat to academics but rather a vehicle for academic content.

Pushing against the notion that play is a frivolous activity, current research based on teaching practices has made connections between academic outcomes and play in its various forms. Multiple studies focus specifically on the positive relationship between dramatic play and academic learning, such as cognition (Gmitrová and Gmitrov 2003; Johnson 2002), as well as specific academic domains like literacy and math (for example, Cook 2000; Marbach and Yawkey 1980; Podlozny 2000; Roskos and Christie 2007). These academic benefits are one of the reasons for the continued privileged position of play in the early childhood classroom and what is considered to be developmentally appropriate practice.

Unfortunately, even as play continues to be theoretically, empirically, and practically valued by those considered most expert in the field, play is less pervasive in practice. Although there have been significant advocacy efforts for a child's right to play over the past few decades, these have not necessarily translated into teaching practices within the current academic climate. Diminishing time for play and shrinking recess periods are all too common in the early childhood classroom (Hirsh-Pasek et al. 2009; Miller and Almon 2009).

This duality—play being important on its own merit, and play as a tool for academic content—places teachers in a unique position in which they must not only decide how to provide for play in the current academic climate but also determine the purpose of the play. Does it have a learning objective? What materials are to be used? Is it time for children to explore independently? Does the teacher engage with the play of their students? Teachers are no longer expected to simply provide space and time for play; they are now considered a key piece in the facilitation of play. Moreover, the teacher's interaction with and around children during play can shape the quality of those play experiences.

Because of these expectations, teachers are faced with important questions and decisions that highlight the many ways they can participate in young children's play and the value that those various interactions can have. To understand this more deeply, we need to take a look back at play from a theoretical perspective. The interconnected relationship between teachers and play has not been constant; rather, it has changed over time depending on the contemporary thinking regarding young children's learning and development. Very often theories on teacher involvement in play stemmed from evolving theoretical stances on *what play is*.

Historically, play was viewed as the pleasurable pastime of young children that was simultaneously educational. In his influential book *Émile, or On Education*, Jean Jacques Rousseau ([1762] 1911) highlighted children's innate ability to learn through their interactions in the world, rather than through books and instruction. By positioning play as the natural activity of young children, Rousseau claimed that rather than placing children's activity under the control of adults, children should be free to explore independently through play. This, Rousseau argued, would be the location for children's development (Bergen 2014; Rousseau [1762] 1911). Johann Pestalozzi (1894) and John Dewey (1910, 1916) both drew from Rousseau's theory, stressing that by allowing children the freedom to explore and play within environments that support children's natural play abilities, self-directed learning through play would occur. The teacher's role was to remain an observer, one whose main purpose was to create an environment in which children could learn independently through play (Bergen 2014; Dewey 1916; Pestalozzi 1894).

Perspectives on children's play from the early to mid-twentieth century focused on the cognitive and social emotional development of children at play. Sigmund Freud (1956) and Jean Piaget (1962) led educational thinking toward understanding children's play as a child-created arena for experimentation and knowledge creation. These theoretical perspectives held the role of teachers at a distance so that the developmental value of play could do its work. According to Piaget's (1962) constructivist approach, just as children grow through specific developmental stages, their play grows in stages as well. Piaget stated that when children play, they are constructing knowledge utilizing their existing cognitive schema. In other words, in play children make meaning of new experiences through the lens of their existing knowledge base; in play they are practicing what they already know (Piaget 1962).

Similarly, Freud (1956) and Erik Erikson (1963) viewed children's play as an act of imaginative creation, in which children rearrange their world into a new, more ordered way. To Freud and Erikson, play was a location for children to face existing anxieties, try on new social roles, and practice and ultimately strengthen their understanding of their own experiences (Bergen 2014; Freud 1956). Freud and Erikson clarified play as the work of children in which they independently experiment with their existing psychological schema (that is, their frame of reference) in order to understand their world.

These theoretical understandings led to a belief that a teacher's presence could disturb children's play and its inherent developmental benefits. This belief that teachers should be bystanders of children's play was reflected via what the field considered to be appropriate practices in the early childhood classroom. In the first version of *Developmentally Appropriate Practice* (Copple and Bredekamp 1986), published by the National Association for the Education of Young Children, Bredekamp states that teachers "prepare the environment so that it provides stimulating challenging materials and activities for children. Then teachers closely observe to see what children understand and pose additional challenges to push their thinking further" (48). During this time, teachers were expected to interact as little as possible in the play of young children.

Lev Vygotsky (1978) identified play as a location in which learning and development meet, but not in a vacuum. Vygotsky thought that the learning and development that occur in play cannot exist without the acknowledgment of cultural-historical context and the presence of other people. Moving beyond the constructivist views of his predecessors, Vygotsky viewed play as a reflection of the external and internal influences in the child's world, as well as a constant source of developmental forward motion.

According to Vygotsky (1978), play has three components: children create an imaginary situation, they take on and act out roles, and they follow specific sets of rules determined by their specific roles. In this particular play context, Vygotsky asserts that play has a hand in the development of children's higher mental functions. Children are able to think symbolically and self-regulate—two higher mental functions not typically within the repertoire of a young child (Bodrova and Leong 2024; Roopnarine and Johnson 2012; Vygotsky 1978). As children play, they are extended into areas of skill and development beyond their current capacity: "Behaving beyond his age, above his usual everyday behavior; in play he is, as it were, a head above himself" (Vygotsky 1978, 74).

This developmental extension is what helps to create a zone of proximal development or ZPD. Vygotsky (1978) claimed that when a child is challenged to acquire certain skills and knowledge that would normally be out of reach, a ZPD is created in which the gap between what a child can do and what a child cannot do becomes much smaller (Meyers and Berk 2014; Vygotsky 1978). Vygotsky never explicitly talked about teacher involvement in play. He did, however, emphasize the ZPD as an area ripe for instruction, and he argued that for instruction to hold the most value, it should be aimed at each individual child's ZPD (Roopnarine and Johnson 2012; Vygotsky 1978).

Current Views on Teachers and Play

Although Vygotsky was not writing from within the current academic climate, over the past twenty years there has been a shift in the way teachers are encouraged to participate in young children's play based on Vygotsky's theoretical understandings. Research and early childhood policy suggest that dramatic play is a way for children to build knowledge, but this process is no longer considered to be a stagnant, solitary act (Bodrova and Leong 2024; NAEYC 2022; Jones and Reynolds 2011). Teachers are no longer expected to simply provide materials and observe children at play, as teachers are now considered an integral part of children's play processes. One reason for this shift in teacher involvement is the emergence of Vygotskian-based curriculum developers who stress the importance of active, intentional teaching.

For example, in their dramatic play-based curriculum, *Tools of the Mind*, Elena Bodrova and Deborah Leong (2024) claim that simply supporting children's play is not enough, and that teachers must actively push play forward by helping to organize the play. This perspective, influenced by Vygotsky's ZPD mentioned previously, establishes that children make advances in their play by interacting dramatically alongside a more skilled player such as the teacher. Similarly, the influence of Vygotsky's theories is also evident in more recent editions of *Developmentally Appropriate Practice*. NAEYC's stance has evolved from the 1986 excerpt mentioned above and currently describes a teacher's intentional play facilitation as such:

> In the dramatic play center, two four-year-old girls are pretending to read menus. Maria (the teacher), noticing that neither girl has taken on the role of waiter, takes notepad and pencil in

hand and asks them, "May I take your order?" Over the next few days, more children join the restaurant play. Waiters set tables, take orders, give orders to the cook, and prepare checks for diners. Maria is an observant, inventive, and intentional teacher. Her intervention sparks fresh play, tempting children to take on different roles, enrich their social and language interactions, and use writing and math for new purposes. (NAEYC 2022; as adapted from Neuman, Copple, and Bredekamp 2000, 52)

Here the teacher joins the play by taking a role in the child-initiated drama, pushing the story forward. From this shared understanding of play in the early childhood classroom, teacher-child interactions are meant to be intentional—carefully thought out based on observations—and also dynamic. Teachers' involvement in play can occur along a wide spectrum, but the one thing these interactions all have in common is the fact that teachers are no longer expected simply to observe but instead are encouraged to engage in and scaffold the play of the children in their classrooms.

As the teacher's involvement in children's play has shifted, so have the ways in which teachers are expected to interpret, provide for, and possibly engage with their students' play. What makes these expectations so unique is the active engagement it requires, beyond simply observing and toward actively thinking about the particular learning goals and differentiated play needs of students.

Teachers inhabit a variety of roles when children play, ranging from outside observers and facilitators to active players (Jones and Reynolds 2011). Outside interventions are defined as opportunities for teachers to extend learning via play from a distance, whereas inside interventions contain strategies to scaffold learning and harness teachable moments. It is within these moments that teachers might enter the play as active participants in the play at hand. An *outsider* supports play without actively participating, and an *insider* enters into and joins the play of children (Smilansky 1968). Although it is a dated classification system for the myriad ways in which teachers engage in play, the early education field does continue to view teacher-child play interactions through this dichotomy. Play facilitations are often categorized by the entry points that teachers choose to engage with, and thus the current research on play contains the "mixed bag" of approaches teachers are dealing with.

The consensus is that whether from outside the play or from within, teachers need to make careful choices about the ways they engage with children, based on their understandings of the play's purpose and their own teaching goals. Thinking about why a teacher takes a specific approach to (or role in) play places the teacher at the forefront of what it means to facilitate play in the early childhood classroom and draws our attention to teachers' own perspectives and beliefs about play: a play pedagogy.

REFLECT

What do you think is the role of play in young children's learning and development? How should teachers be involved?

How do you see your role as an educator in the play of young children?

CHAPTER 2

Play and Pedagogy

WHEN WE BECOME TEACHERS, we need the knowledge and expertise to be effective as educators. A history teacher needs to be well versed in history. A math teacher needs to be familiar with math. It is well documented that children learn best through play, so a large part of early childhood content is play based. As early childhood educators, play should be our area of expertise!

The definition of play is frequently contested, one that evolves with the perspectives and purposes of the definer. Brian Sutton-Smith (1997) referred to "the ambiguity of play" when trying to pin down a definition. Is it playing games with rules? Is it exploration or creation? Is it always joyful and done for pleasure? Is it intrinsically motivated? The questions go on and on. Perhaps the trouble in defining it comes from the fact that the motivation, action, and rules around play shift and change according to the context at hand. For the purposes of our work here, play will be considered timeless and fluid, occurring both in childhood and adulthood. To me, the simpler the definition, the better. Play is an action or activity that is outside the parameters of everyday life; an action that holds no external purpose (for the player) besides the act of playing or creating.

Play is the foundation of all early childhood learning and development, so early childhood teachers should be confident with their play knowledge. In this chapter, we will explore play and its participants, further developing our play knowledge into a way of knowing, or a play pedagogy, that we carry into the classroom every day.

On a daily basis, teachers are making important decisions about how to incorporate and allow for play into the lives of their students: what types of play to offer, how much time to dedicate to play, even what level of involvement they themselves should have in the play of their students. Beyond making the daily logistic decisions about play in the classroom, teachers also need to assess the play at hand and establish what their role is within that play at any given time. To join the play or to simply observe?

Regardless of the roles we may take up (from outside the play or from within), teachers need to make careful choices about the ways they engage with children based on their understandings of the play's purpose and their own teaching goals. But what is the basis of these decisions? Thinking about *why* we take a specific approach to our role in play places the teacher at the forefront of understanding what it means to facilitate play in the early childhood classroom and draws our attention to teachers' own perspectives and beliefs about the value of play— that is, their play pedagogy.

REFLECT

How would *you* define play? (It's harder than you'd think!)

Where do/would you fit within the play of the children in your classroom? Would you join the play, or would you be more comfortable observing?

What roles do you see other teachers utilizing that you find yourself drawn to?

Play Pedagogy

Pedagogy is a system of knowledge and beliefs about education that is both practical and theoretical. In the simplest of terms, it is the act of educating and a way of knowing about teaching and learning. It is the how and why teachers do what they do and the foundation from which teachers make decisions for the students in their classroom. Pedagogy not only informs our practice but has a part in shaping our teacher identity and how we see our role in the classroom.

As mentioned earlier, a teacher's play pedagogy is the practical expression of their personal and practical knowledge about play in the early childhood classroom (Ryan and Northey-Berg 2014). This sweet spot is the intersection of **who I am** and **what I know**—the culmination of a lifetime of experiences with play both personal and professional. Every teacher brings this way of knowing into their classroom every day, an amalgamation of not only skills learned in teacher education programs but also personal experiences, memories, and values.

Who I Am

Play is a phenomenon that is simultaneously universal and extraordinarily personal, a shared experience that we all have as humans. Yet when examined more deeply, play is very specific, as it reflects our sociocultural contexts on many levels. These individualized experiences are often shaped by the geographical, cultural, and social environments in which we grow.

A lifetime of experiencing play begins in childhood. Whether it is through playing games in the street outside, playing house, or exploring in the woods, without knowing it, teachers begin to develop the core values of their own play pedagogy early on, beginning with their experiences with play as children. As we grow, we build an understanding of the self as it pertains to playful activity. What we like to play and what we don't like to play both have a part in shaping our playful life throughout childhood.

In adulthood, play may change, but it still finds a way. There are many ways of engaging with play as an adult, be it playing games on your phone, acting with a community theater, playing in a softball league, having a weekly poker game, attending an art class, or going to a trivia night. Free time as an adult is fleeting, so how we choose to spend it is worth looking at. When we engage our playful side in a world that doesn't always lend itself to adult play, we are making a choice for ourselves that has resonance. These adult play experiences add to an already existing understanding of play, furthering the development of a play pedagogy.

The way someone experiences play throughout their lifetime has a lasting impact on their personal values and beliefs about play. When considering who we are as educators, we cannot ignore the play experiences that have shaped us into practitioners with preconceived notions of what play looks like. By exploring this key part of our history, we continue to shape **who I am**; the identity of someone who plays.

What I Know

Professional knowledge is gained from external experiences. The way teachers are taught about play and the way play is regarded in the workplace are crucial pieces in the development of a pedagogy of play. In having these experiences, teachers take in information and make it their own, ripening an ownership of what play means. It is the shaping of **what I know** to be true about play.

From teacher preparation courses to professional development, teachers and teachers-to-be are asked not just to think about play in the theoretical sense but to think about play as a way of interacting with the young children in their classroom. In learning to develop curriculum for young children, teachers gain an understanding of how and when play is to be incorporated into early childhood settings, what materials are to be used, and how this play is valuable for young children's growth and development. Although these understandings are varied because of the different ways in which teacher preparation programs approach play and play-based learning, they universally have impact. How teachers are taught to interpret and facilitate for play in a classroom becomes a part of their play pedagogy (see, for example, Bauml 2011; Logue and Harvey 2010), and this knowledge helps teachers to formulate a deeper understanding of play's purpose in the classroom.

Once the educator is in the classroom, their play pedagogy grows as they take their educational experiences with play and put them to practical use. Teachers make important decisions rooted in what they have learned in teacher preparation programs, as well as through their own experiences as classroom teachers.

A play pedagogy based in practice also is informed by the environments in which teachers teach, as the set of beliefs or values about play that are held by the school as an institution has an influence on how teachers think about and enact their own play pedagogy. The degree to which play is valued in a particular school's academic culture and, more broadly, in national policy, has a place in the development of teachers' play pedagogy. A school whose administration values academics and school readiness will have a collective play pedagogy that is very different from a school whose administration recognizes and fosters the inherent value of play.

When we are examining both who we are and what we know as it pertains to play, we are continuing to develop a larger conceptual understanding of the word. Play pedagogy that stems from these ways of knowing is not stagnant; rather, it is a fluid work in progress that grows with the individual. We are finding the space where our past and present experiences with play—both personal and professional—combine, developing a deeper, more holistic understanding of what play is and should be. Teachers' pedagogical choices as they pertain to play are both driven by and a result of this conceptualization of play. These modalities for thinking and talking about play are the embodiment of the influences in teachers' lives, a way of evaluating play through multiple lenses, and ultimately informers of a teacher's play pedagogy.

REFLECT

What are some of the basic tenets of your play pedagogy?

_____

_____

_____

_____

What do you know to be true about play?

_____

_____

_____

_____

CHAPTER 3

Reflection
Play Stories

WE TAKE AN UNDERSTANDING of play into our classrooms every day, based on our experiences as teachers but also based on our experiences as human beings. These experiences (and our interpretation of them) are naturally existing wells of knowledge—who we are and what we know. But if we don't acknowledge them as such, they can be left untapped and unexamined. When we take stock of these parts of our pedagogy and dip into the wells of personal and practical knowledge, we become more well-rounded, multidimensional practitioners.

But how do we gain access to these deep, meaningful aspects of our teaching? Reflection! Reflective teaching is typically a self-evaluative tool in which teachers observe their own practice: what works, what doesn't, and why. Most reflective practices in education involve looking back on your teaching, or *reflection on action*, as well as evaluating your teaching in the moment, or *reflection in action* (Dewey 1933; Schön 1983). These formats of reflection are focused on the practices of the teacher and the performance of the students. They help teachers understand the impact that their teaching is having on the classroom as a whole and are inherently *outward*-looking forms of reflection.

In addition to these practice-based formats for teacher reflection, there are certain types of *inward* reflection that allow us to look at our teaching through the lens of our own experiences. Thinking about our experiences in this way carves a space for us to consider our teaching as specific and personal (Pinar 1981).

REFLECT

How do you reflect on your teaching? What motivates these reflections? What form do they take?

Play Stories

Play stories are a valuable format for teacher reflection and self-assessment. Through the process of creating a play story, teachers can engage in inward-focused reflection that is geared toward increasing awareness and facilitating pedagogical change. This reflection is not *in action* or *on action*, but rather it is reflection *on past* (Clark 2019), using personal history as a means of reflection. Instead of simply looking outward at our teaching practice, let us look inward and consider our past experiences as informers of our current teaching practice.

The term *play story* is not limited only to childhood memories; rather, it can be further clarified as memories of and experiences with play as children, as young adults, and as grown practitioners. Creating a play story is an autobiographical act that chronicles an individual's experience with play, starting with childhood and expanding into adult play and teacher play. Developing a play story requires that we look backward and forward, at our past and our present, through a play lens.

This book reflects the power of play stories as a tool for understanding our practice. Four play stories were lovingly cocreated by myself and the participants of my 2017 dissertation study, "Play Then and Now: A Narrative Study of Early Childhood Teachers' Play Histories and Practices." I worked alongside four preschool teachers to evoke memories of the past and to carry those memories into our conversations about practice. After conducting the play story interviews, I re-storied their play time line into chronological order, highlighting two phases of play experience: the *child at play* and the *teacher at play*. In addition, I wove in my observations of each of the teachers during free play in their classrooms. After the play stories were completed, I began to look across the experiences to see what commonalities were shared by all of the participants who took part in this project (these will be discussed in later chapters).

Discussing a history with play with these four women was remarkable. The teachers would get lost in the telling: some closing their eyes to evoke a feeling, some laughing about the ridiculousness of certain play scenarios, some lamenting about the play of their youth. Singularly and as a group, the teachers (prompted by the storytelling process) shared a history with play that began with rich, meaningful childhood memories and ended with experiences playing alongside the children in their classrooms. All of their names have been changed for privacy purposes.

All four of the teachers I spoke with about their memories of play had similar reactions. No matter the background, no matter the context, when I spoke with the teachers about their childhood play, something lit up inside them. Each interview began with a prompt asking the teachers to walk me through their childhood home. As each teacher took me on this journey, they shared smiles and laughter as they told me about the special locations for their play, spots that only a child knows—a branch of a tree, a basement, a barn, a cozy armchair. In describing these spaces for play, the teachers conjured memories of times long forgotten and the feelings that went along with them.

The connections to and ideas about their childhoods were a driving force in discussing how they regard the practice of play and held a mirror up to their classroom practice. As you will read, Kara's thoughtful facilitations, Megan's quiet, meticulous work, Sara's creations, and Jane's unbridled joy for play all are pieces of a very particular set of play skills. These skills that every teacher inherently possesses are a valuable asset to the many play scenarios that young children find themselves in on a daily basis in school.

REFLECT

Play stories are a tribute to the varied lives of teachers and the multitude of ways in which people experience play. As you read the following stories, I ask you to notice what they bring about for you regarding your own experiences. What feelings surface when you read about the play experiences of others? What commonalities do you share? What differences do you note?

CHAPTER 4

The Puzzler

The child at play. *It is Sunday. Megan is tucked away in a corner of her grandparents' apartment in a major city. She has come into the city with her mother and sister to go to church, but now, finally, she is able to sit down and play with her grandparents' Matryoshka doll. The kitchen is noisy, filled with sounds of food being prepared and animated discussions in Russian, but Megan has found a quiet space. She peers at the doll, an old man holding a staff, whom she imagines is a priest or a monk. Opening the nesting dolls one by one, Megan sticks her nose deep inside their halves to breathe in the musty yet comforting smell. She then lines the re-formed dolls next to one another, from largest to smallest. Megan leans back and admires her work, smiling.*

MEGAN WAS BORN IN 1961 in a small town in South America, although her story does not begin there. Megan's grandparents were born to nobility at the time of the Russian Revolution in Moscow. As life in Russia became more complicated, Megan's family moved gradually westward, landing in Austria, where Megan's mother was born. Eventually the work of her grandfather brought the family to Argentina and then a coastal town in Peru where Megan would eventually be born. A year and a half later, the entire family moved to a large city in the United States; Megan's sister was born soon after, tucked into a stroller that would roll across the slanted apartment floor. They lived there for only a brief time, but it was full of experiences with extended family, grandparents and great-grandparents alike. Megan recalls eating aromatic chestnuts with her grandfather. Megan lived with her family in the city until she was around the age of four, and at that point Megan, her mother, and her younger sister moved to a small town in a county just north of the city that held a strong Russian Orthodox population. Home, or "the bungalow" as Megan fondly called it, was a tiny house on a busy street in the northern part of town that spread along a large river. The house had a huge backyard facing down the hill toward the river, with trees for climbing and space for her mother to plant a garden.

A majority of Megan's play life existed in the areas in and around her home. She shared many of these play experiences with her sister (who was younger by two and a half years) in the hours after school. After-noon activities were left up to the girls because their mother worked two jobs and would typically be gone until the evening. After coming home on the bus, Megan and her sister would make their way along the busy road that led to their house, carefully ambling behind the guard-rail to avoid oncoming traffic. Once home, they would check in with their mother on the phone, "forage" for snack, and then get down to the business of play.

Dolls were a priority. Due to their mother's discomfort with Barbie's physique, the girls would play with Casey and Francine, Barbie's less-endowed cousins. Megan and her sister would create play scenarios in which the dolls had dates with John and David, the resident teddy bear boyfriends, because their mother wouldn't allow Ken dolls in the house. In our conversations, Megan often said that doll play was her preferred form of dramatic play with her sister. She claimed she did not have the imagination or patience for pretend play in which she would take on a role. Although sometimes she would go along with whatever story her sister wanted to play out, it was not something she remem-bered enjoying:

I cannot stand pretend play. My sister was very much into pretend play herself. She would dress up in scarves and put tights on her head, and those were her long pigtails—she had a wild imagination. And she just played whimsically by herself because I rarely, rarely joined in. If I did, it was with the dolls.

Megan would sometimes acquiesce and go along with her sister's dramatic play scenarios, for example, becoming a teacher because "she was the eldest," dragging out books, crayons, and papers to hold class. She often described their shared dramatic play as "directed" by her sister, who typically demanded to be a ballerina in any given dramatic context.

Megan also found great joy in other types of play. Although she had fond memories of running around outside and climbing the trees in her yard, as well as a profound love of snow, she characterized her most pleasing childhood play scenarios as quiet and indoors. She discussed her love of books and puzzles quite often, describing her family as a group of puzzlers:

We were a very wordy family; we loved puzzles. Very, very big on jigsaw puzzles—that was from my grandmother. My mother, myself, and my sister were all incredibly, almost obsessed jigsaw puzzlers. Yeah, very good at it.

A lot of the play that Megan enjoyed as a child could be described as cerebral. She gleefully described a particular week home sick from school during which her mother would go to the library after work and bring home armloads of books. There, sick on the couch, she would devour the books one by one and await the next delivery from her mother, who also happened to be a "big reader" as well.

In our time together, Megan shaped the identity of a player who was influenced by family, captivated by certain activities and repelled by others—a childhood spent within her particular context—developing opinions, preferences, and ultimately choices about how she chose to play.

REFLECT

Think back to where you spent the majority of your childhood. What were the spaces your found yourself playing in? It could be outdoors or indoors. Try to remember the details of the space. Describe some of the toys/play materials you would encounter there. What did you play in these spaces?

_____

_____

_____

_____

_____

_____

_____

_____

_____

The teacher at play. _Megan approaches a table with three young children and a pile of lids and caps. She settles in quietly next to them and "takes in" the materials in front of her. "I like to be able to see all the caps," she says. Megan is organizing, experimenting, and playing alongside them as they chat about various things: her kids, food, the caps, and so on. She has created a rainbow of caps—arranging them according to color. "Here's my rainbow! Red, orange, yellow, green, blue, purple." I find out later that Megan collected all of these recyclable items (hundreds of colorful caps and lids that fill a laundry basket) from her home. As I observe Megan in the classroom, she spends a good ten to fifteen minutes at this table quietly chatting and organizing lids and caps. She engages children in her play by asking questions and conducting her own experiments: "Which [lid] will hit the table first?" "Oh! You know what I like about this? The sound. . . . That [lid] is the loudest, and . . . (whispers) that [lid] is the quietest." Megan has found a seat at this table in_ *which she seems to genuinely engage with the materials in a curious and playful way. She begins to create a tower of the lids, and as she builds she narrates her actions to the children around her, who are watching in awe. "I'm trying to see how far I can stack it before it falls down. It looks a little wobbly, but it's still standing up. . . . If you race while you build, it will fall down . . . . You build with slow, careful movements." Even as Megan leaves the table to attend to other classroom business, the children continue to experiment with the unique materials she has provided them. Later Megan will join the table again and return to her studious, quiet, intentional play work.*

Though Megan graduated with a bachelor's degree in math and economics, she discovered early on that banking was not for her. On a whim, she took an assistant teaching position at a nursery school and immediately fell in love with teaching. She enrolled in a teaching program and graduated within one calendar year. When I asked Megan to reflect on her education and how play and early childhood were presented to her as a graduate student, she shared that she was involved in a program that was considered "liberal" at the time. Her schooling focused on educating the whole child with an emphasis on play—a philosophy she carries with her still:

> It's about meeting the child where they are, following their interests, sparking their creativity, their love of learning, their love of books. . . . I like working with the little ones—it's all about learning how to be a person, a good friend, a. . . . You know, it's not really all about learning your ABCs.

Before landing at her current position, Megan took various teaching jobs in private preschools and substitute teaching positions, all the while raising a family. She has been teaching at this school full-time for the past four years. Megan is the head teacher in the three- to five-year-old after-school program at the school. The model of the program requires a themed curriculum, and that planning lands with Megan. The afternoon begins outside in the play yard, with the class later moving indoors for a circle time activity and then to various play centers.

Every time I enter the classroom, I am struck by the calm that Megan exudes during circle time. The children are watching carefully as she shows them a book about salamanders. "I used to catch bright orange salamanders at camp when I was little," she says while leaning over to give a child a closer look at a picture. Later, as the children have made their way to various play centers, Megan moves slowly from table to table, making commentary on the play that is happening and eventually settling down with some waffle blocks. "You see how the waffle blocks have three sticks on one end and two on the other? The three side always sticks with the two side." She shows a child how to get them to fit together. "See? Now it fits perfectly."

She later shared, "I guess it's an interest in physics. I love building with them. I love playing marbles with them. Those are the things I enjoy. And sorting and playing with manipulatives. That's my thing." Megan's interest in puzzles, games, and building was apparent in most of her interactions I observed in the classroom. She was quick to share her strategy for organizing puzzle pieces by edges and shapes, admire how a child was sorting manipulatives, or help a child build a structure that could contain little play animals.

As Megan discussed her role as a teacher at play, she continued to express a dislike of dramatic play in which she has to take on a role:

> I don't like pretend play. It makes me crazy, and when students of mine say, "Pretend you're the momma cat and blah, blah," I'm like, "No, go find your own friends to play momma cat." I just don't like it. I don't have the patience for it, I guess, I don't know why. I mean, I don't want to squash their thoughts and things, but I don't feel like that's my job to do with them.

This sentiment was evident in her classroom practice as well. She maintained a strong presence in many of the other areas of the classroom but did not seem to engage with children in the dramatic play area of the classroom unless necessary. For example, when two children began to play in the kitchen area of the dramatic play corner and eventually found themselves having a sword fight with two fake "spears" of asparagus, Megan reminded them, "We don't really like to play with swords at school—it's dangerous," and moved on. Although Megan was not an active participant in the dramatic play in the classroom, she was keenly aware of what was going on. A child put on a pair of star-shaped sunglasses, to which Megan exclaimed, "Oh you look like a movie star!"

Megan is a confident, warm, engaging teacher. She clearly has a preference for what she chooses to engage with in the classroom. Megan's fondest childhood play memories represented a very particular type of play—but even more significant, her narrative radiated warmth, pride, and history.

REFLECT

Which play activities in the classroom do you find yourself truly enjoying/getting lost in? Why do you think that is?

CHAPTER 5

The Character

The child at play. *It is well past noon, and Jane has been in a tree for hours. High in the Japanese maple in her yard, Jane peers down at the ground and kicks her sneakers off—they fly to the grass below and land with a thud. Now, unencumbered by footwear, she maneuvers from branch to branch and, ignoring her mother's demands to stay low in the tree, climbs higher. Pretending to be Barney the dinosaur (a popular childhood television icon), who also happens to be fighting off pirates, she yells at imaginary enemies, threatening them with walking the plank to certain death. With the grace that only a six-year-old has when climbing a tree, Jane makes her way to her "perfect spot" and settles herself against the curve of the trunk of the tree that fits her precisely. She digs into her shorts and pulls out a little plastic container that holds Polly Pocket, a miniature doll that has stretchy clothes for dressing it. She quietly dresses and undresses her a few times before becoming aware of the approaching pirate ship, and so she prepares for battle.*

JANE WAS BORN IN 1992 in a suburban area outside a major US city. Her parents were twenty-one and twenty-five when she was born, and they separated soon after, when Jane was around six months old. Throughout her childhood, Jane's time was split between two locations, often moving from house to house. "About every year of my life, I moved, whether it was with my dad or my mom or both of them." Jane spent the weekdays with her mother in various locations in the suburbs around the city, and eventually she spent weekends with her father about an hour away beyond the state border. These two locations became the space for two very different childhood experiences. Jane often discussed their contrast, not only in the physical environments in which her childhood occurred but also in the ways her parents interacted with her and the social relationships she developed in each area.

Most of Jane's time with her mother was spent in and around their home and in the thickly settled part of their street, with houses situated quite close to one another. Jane's mother eventually remarried when Jane was around eight years old; the family was joined by her brother when she was ten and her sister about two years later. From kindergarten to the middle of second grade, Jane attended a school where she not only felt like she belonged as a social member of the play community but also identified herself as a leader within the play lives of the neighborhood children:

> I was known as the little mayor of [name of school]. I remember on the playground, with all the kids—you know they start to form their cliques? And I remember telling everybody, I was like, "I'm playing with everybody. You guys want to play with each other like that? Go play by yourself. Otherwise, we're all playing together."

Jane often discussed her mother's choice to switch her from the local public school to the Catholic school in the area, and the impact of that shift. When discussing the move, Jane shared memories about the difficulties she faced and the challenges of integrating into an already established social system. Jane shared that the girls had already formed cliques that she found hard to penetrate.

The play experiences that took place at her mother's house were primarily solitary in nature or involved a small group of friends. Jane's mother worked multiple jobs at various times in her childhood, so often Jane was left to play on her own. She recalled waking up and getting her own bottle from the refrigerator and putting in a favorite VHS tape to watch while her mother slept in after a late night at work. She described her mother as strict and somewhat of a worrier. For these reasons, the play that occurred at her mother's was often close to home.

Every Friday, Jane's father would pick her up in the early evening, and she would spend the weekend in the landscape of a different kind of suburbia. Sprawling lawns and a sea of housing developments perched on an isolated hill provided ample space for Jane to explore on her bike alongside her neighbors. Jane's father was much more lenient when it came to her play activities: "My dad was a bachelor and had his daughter come every weekend, so he was kind of like, you know, he's taking a break too. 'Go do whatever the hell you want. I don't care.'" It was here where Jane's social play relationships became much more important and something to depend on. "Because I moved around a lot more at my mom's, I didn't have that group to kind of go back to. Every weekend, I had that group at my dad's house to go to. I knew that later I'd be playing with Holly and Beth." Jane described the joy of knocking on doors to see who could come to play, riding bikes, and exploring the neighborhood with groups of children until dinnertime.

These two distinctly different play environments shaped Jane's memories in a significant way, but the play that happened in these spaces did not differ greatly. Jane's connections to the imaginative world and the characters that inhabited it were constant in her memories of childhood play. Dramatic play with dolls, as well as taking on roles from popular media, were a huge part of Jane's play life no matter which parent she was staying with. "Barbies. Barbies. Period, end of story. I was a Barbie girl." Jane described all the various ways in which she would use the Barbies as characters from popular media and act out scenes while watching television. "You know, I mean I'd be playing, but the TV would be on too. So, we're playing with my Barbies—we'd have our own thing going on—but *Boy Meets World* would be on too or whatever. So maybe they'd become Angela and Topanga (characters from the show) or something." Jane's play with Barbies or Polly Pockets often represented characters from movies or television—"her playmate" that she was watching at that moment. The Barbies would have fashion shows or have a girls' day and laze about the giant three-story Barbie Dreamhouse that Jane owned.

When spending time with the neighborhood children at her father's house or playing alone at either parent's home, characters from popular media were represented in Jane's imaginative play. More often than not, Jane chose to take on a role from current movies and television. "I've noticed that . . . I'm very movie and TV . . . [and] a lot of my play comes from what I've seen and stuff like that." Whether Jane was using a bow and arrow as her father taught her to pretend to be Legolas from *The Lord of the Rings* movies or dressed in full costume as Queen Amidala from the *Star Wars* movies, preparing for a lightsaber battle, Jane's connection to media had a considerable impact on the ways in which she engaged in dramatic play as a child. "I watched movies way too much. No, honestly, way too much. I would pretend to be different characters in the different movies, depending on who I was with. I mean, if I was by myself, it didn't matter. I would play anything— I really didn't care."

As Jane's play interests shifted, she began to play more with another type of media: video games. Her father was "really into computers" and taught Jane how to navigate games like *The Oregon Trail* and *Where in the World Is Carmen Sandiego?* She described that impact of spending time lost in a computer game and the joy she felt while engaged in an alternate reality. As she aged out of those types of games, Jane became interested in *The Sims*, a life-simulation computer game in which you create an environment with characters in it and play around with these characters within an established setting. Jane connected with the game on both an imaginative and creative level; she was hooked:

> There was one time where my mom—six hours went by and she was like, "Dinner's ready." And I was like, "What? Dinner, already?" And she was like, "Yeah. What have you been doing in the basement?" And I was like, "I've been playing *The Sims*." She's like, "The whole time? Six hours you were playing a computer game?"

Jane talked about how her mother limited her access to the game, whereas her father allowed her to play as much as she wanted, which was a lot. Jane mentioned that even now as an adult, she enjoys the game—"I downloaded it immediately, and I still play that. I have so much fun with it." Jane's love of character play found a happy home in the "virtual dollhouse" world of *The Sims*. When Jane interacted with technology or other types of media, these interactions were based on a fascination and a love for the characters in the stories.

Jane shared with me her love of dramatic play. Through dolls, miniatures, role play, and gaming, Jane's character play was usually defined by characters found in popular media. Jane's capacity to find playful inspiration in the characters and stories she was exposed to is a representation of the play environments she found herself in throughout her childhood, coupled with an aptitude for dramatic play.

REFLECT

What did you absolutely love to play? Whom did you play with? Why was this play so special to you?

What types of play do you remember disliking in your childhood? Why did this type of play not interest you?

The teacher at play. *Dinner is served in the dramatic play area. Jane is seated, awaiting her meal. Children surround her, furiously rummaging through the various spaces where play food is kept. The sounds of busy meal prep fill the room: plastic plates clattering against one another, waitresses discussing the customers' choices with the cooks, and Jane making demands. A child rushes a cup of pretend water over to her. "Water? That's it? I'm hungry!" Jane is simultaneously playing and socializing/talking with coteachers and myself. Somehow, it is established that they are eating in the desert. A student teacher seems to try to push the play a bit by asking for a table for one. Jane doesn't pick up that offer—and continues with her storyline: "I think I might need gallons of water. . . . What am I eating today? Dinner? Can I have some chicken and potatoes and green beans?" Jane's commitment to the drama at hand is impressive, to the point where I can't help but wonder if this is how Jane behaves in real restaurants: "What am I eating? Just a bun? Okay . . . can I have some butter? It's a little dry." Jane is genuinely invested in the meal at hand, and the children are thrilled.*

Jane's path to teaching had always been fairly clear. As a young girl, Jane was often drawn to her teachers as social partners rather than to the children in her class. She would often remove herself from school activities to sit with the teachers, watching them carefully and hoping to take over. She recalled thinking, "Oh, I can do this. . . . This I can definitely do." And she could. She trained as a teacher at a local community college and honed her practice through a variety of impactful field placements in and around the area. Although her schooling took a bit longer than expected because "life took over," Jane found that she was comforted by simply walking into a classroom. "Every time I walked into the classroom with kids, I could put life aside, and I was just *in* with the kids. I was all kid, you know, all the time. . . . I want to be in there. I want to be engaged and everything." After achieving her associate degree, this energy and engagement with children, coupled with good timing, led her to securing her current job.

In discussing the role of play in the early childhood classroom, Jane briefly identified the philosophical similarities between her teacher training and her current place of employment—specifically, "play being the center of all learning." But primarily when Jane explored the role of play in the classroom, she mostly talked about her commitment to and engagement with children at play. Jane related to herself as a dramatic player, showcasing the ease with which she not only engages with the dramatic play of young children but *enjoys it*:

> I feel like play totally defined me, and it still kind of does because I am a player. I don't like to sit back and watch, unless I'm tired, but I like to be like totally involved with the kids. . . . And I really enjoy it, you know? I really do. I like getting silly. I like being funny with these guys and everything and go home when the day is done, but we all had a good day and it was really fun.

Jane's ability to commit to the dramatic reality of the children's restaurant play in the passage above demonstrates her capacity for full play engagement, taking up the offerings of the children and therefore investing deeply in their play. This investment has its own sort of payoff; the children swarm to Jane while she plays—they are entranced by this adult figure who is picking up the plotline of their play and extending it, not for any academic purpose or to direct their play, but for the sheer enjoyment of the play itself.

〰〰〰〰〰〰〰〰〰〰〰〰〰〰〰〰〰〰〰〰〰〰〰〰〰〰〰〰

Jane is lying on the rug with a child, building a house for miniature frog figurines. "I have to protect my frogs from predators," Jane says as she builds a wall out of blocks around her frog house. All of a sudden, a child roars a loud, threatening call, alarming the architect. "Oh my goodness, dinosaurs are here—I don't know if my frogs will be safe in the house—uh-oh, there goes the roof!" The child's eyes widen and his face breaks into an ecstatic grin as he begins to slowly stomp closer and closer toward Jane's structure. Jane is nervously gathering her frogs around her and building a wall as fast as she can, as three more children join in the dinosaur's path of destruction. They are vibrating with excitement. They attack: "Oh my goodness! Yikes! He just pulled my house apart! My frogs better wake up! My froggies are getting eaten! Oh, hop away, hop away!"

〰〰〰〰〰〰〰〰〰〰〰〰〰〰〰〰〰〰〰〰〰〰〰〰〰〰〰〰

The characters from popular media that fascinated Jane so deeply as a child remain significant for her still, both in and outside of the classroom. Her knowledge of current child-based media has come to be a source of pride for Jane as an educator, something that makes her stand out from the other teachers and a valuable authority for character play. "They'll [the children] talk about a movie and I'll do the quote from the movie because I just know that movie really well. So then I'm pretending to be whatever character that was." Jane's character knowledge in its various forms and her eagerness to engage in this type of play is rooted in her past and evident in her preferences for classroom play—"I relate to it," she says.

REFLECT

As a play facilitator, what classroom play activities do you find yourself avoiding? Why do you think that is?

CHAPTER 6

The Explorer

The child at play. *Kara is running. She is running through the woods as fast as her seven-year-old feet will carry her. Her lungs are burning as she sucks in the air around her. Tearing through the brambles, Kara pays no mind to the massive amounts of burdocks getting stuck to her sweater and focuses on her footsteps, one, two, three, four, the cadence of a horse galloping. The smell of moss, dirt, and rotting logs leaves her nose as she approaches the hill behind her house and her expectant mother, who has called them all in for dinner. Turning back quickly, she catches a glimpse of her brothers, who are gaining on her in the unspoken race to get to the dinner table first. She is slightly disappointed that they have been called in (even if they had been out all day), mainly due to the fact that they had decided to climb up onto the roof of the tree house the boys had built, a first for this group. She quickly brushes away the disappointment and pays it no mind, because now she is a horse. She vibrates her lips, rears up, and thunders down the hill for what smells like meat loaf.*

BORN TO A EUROPEAN MOTHER and a father serving overseas in the US military, Kara's roots run deep in two very different parts of the world. She was born in Europe in 1951, the first girl, joining her parents and two older brothers. A large portion of her family's early years were spent all across Europe, with each child born in a different location, until they ultimately landed in a major European city for the birth of the fourth and final child, another girl. They stayed there through Kara's first year of kindergarten and then headed to the United States, landing in a rural part of the Northeast near her father's family.

The house where the family lived for most of Kara's childhood was built in the 1700s. The house with a small stable for horses rested atop a hill on three and a half acres a few miles out of town. Their home was surrounded by a thickly wooded area that was a source of great joy for Kara: deep woods for hiking in, filled with skunk cabbage and marshland for mucking around, ponds for skating, and a tree house built by her brothers.

A large majority of Kara's childhood play was located outdoors. Warm-weather days were spent deep in the woods surrounding the house. Winter days found her skating on ponds and building snow dragons and snow forts. She mentioned on multiple occasions that she was a member of the generation that was told to "go out and play," sent out for the day, and not expected back in the house except for meals. She often reminisced about the innocence of this time and remarked that kids don't play that way anymore, reflecting about how things don't seem as safe and also how there has been a shift in the way that parents allow their children to play. This acknowledgment of the passage of time and nostalgia for the way things used to be often led her to compare her childhood to the lives of her students. "Never would I allow that in today's world. But it's different. But we had free rein. The four of us could go off in the woods by ourselves. My parents thought nothing of that." Kara lamented that children today would never be given the freedoms she had, walking deep into the woods, learning to swim simply by jumping in the water, and taking on jobs.

Kara, alongside her sister and two brothers, also spent time playing in the horse stable "doing chores." Like their father, all the children were riders in the local horse club run by their grandmother and were expected to pitch in and care for the horses, Beauty and Dixie. These chores were transformed (as they often are by children) into play scenarios:

Those stables had to be mucked and mucked. But we loved playing up above. You'd go up a little ladder, and you're up in the hay bales. That was fun. We'd hide in there—a lot of hide-and-seek and that kind of thing. . . . We would climb on the roof and then jump in if there was hay or straw available. Sometimes there was manure fights. You were a little gamey. I mean, you can never forget why you took so many baths. Well, that was why. My mother was like, "Ew."

The kids would often watch as the horses were cared for. Kara had a stump that she liked to sit on while she watched the farrier work or chatted with the woman who came to braid the horses' manes before a show. The horses, and the activities around the work to keep them, became a source of playfulness for Kara and her siblings, and often a theme in her play. She recalls putting on her father's huge riding boots and flopping around in the house in them, as well as making her Barbies ride toy horses. This identification of her family as a group of "horse people" was a common theme throughout Kara's discussion of her childhood, and it was reflected in the way she talked about her activities (both playful and work related) and her connections to her older family members like her father and grandmother.

Outside where they had "free rein," the explorers set to work; Kara talked about how playing with her brothers was always an exciting adventure. Crashing through the woods alongside her brothers and sister, pretending to be animals or explorers, hopping rocks, and getting into some "very active play" was a typical day in the wild with her siblings. Wherever her brothers went, she wanted to go too, and whatever they could do, she could do too, even if it meant some risky play:

> There was a lot of roughhousing with the brothers. Then they'd get bored with each other, and they would come after my sister and me. If they did something we didn't like—well, "I'm going to tell"—then we were called tattletalers. But that seemed to be our only defense because they were just bigger and stronger—a lot of rough-and-tumble play.

In the summer, the family would head north to the family camp in the mountains, and the outdoor adventures continued. Kara shared vivid descriptions of summers on the lake, learning to swim ("I'm talking not where today everything is so structured and you get swimming lessons") and canoeing with her father. The camp was rustic: washing clothes on a washboard in the lake, using outhouses, and keeping the food cold in an icehouse during the warmer months. Far from any semblance of a town, the four children were kept busy canoeing, swimming in the freezing water, and jumping precariously onto rocks along the shoreline. Kara and her younger sister slept in the "far" cabin, holding hands while they drifted off to the sound of peepers and the water lapping at the shore of the lake.

Although Kara talked of other types of play, including playing Barbies with her sister and putting on shows, pretending to be Marilyn Monroe, a large part of our conversations revolved around the outdoors and the adventures that took place there.

REFLECT

Outside of your home, where did you play? The woods? The neighborhood? What kinds of play occurred in those locations?

The teacher at play. *Kara is in the dramatic play area, which is staged like a tent. She is covered in children. They are cozied up to her as she flips through the pages of a book about the desert, pointing out the different pictures and making commentary. "Don't lean too close to this picture!" she exclaims, pointing to a picture of a cactus. She pretends to be pricked by the cactus in the book: "Ow! Is there a first aid kit? It's getting red and bumpy! I need water to put on it." A child scurries off to get water but is distracted by the group of children forming under the tent, preparing to go to sleep. They are squealing with the excitement that goes along with playing under a sheet. "Snuggle city!" Kara says. She takes up their storyline and extends it to the theme of the play area: "It's getting cold. Do we need a blanket? A sandstorm is coming; it's blowing on the tent roof." The children's eyes widen as she covers them all up by floating an additional sheet up and over their bodies. The scene is very cozy looking. "Good night," she whispers and backs away from the play.*

Kara began her academic path studying design in a large city before she soon realized that it was not for her—the noise and the people were too much: "I'm not a city person, which I found out loud and clear through living in the city!" She ended up attending a state university close to home, graduating with a bachelor's degree in art education. At that point, Kara shifted her focus to family and had three children but continued to take classes throughout that period. When her youngest child was in nursery school, Kara took a part-time substitute job at a lab school at a small nearby college and was asked to join the school full- time. She said yes, enrolled her daughter at the school, and continued on to finish her master's degree in early childhood education. She has taught at this school, this book's study site, ever since.

In talking with Kara about play and the curricular philosophies she encountered in her teacher training, she often mentioned the types of roles that children take on in their dramatic play. She highlighted these roles as a reflection of their worlds, for example, children pretending to be a parent or a well-known community archetype like a police officer or a postal worker:

I always thought it was kind of interesting, because you go in the dramatic play area, and the children take on the roles of . . . their parents . . . [or] what they see happening. It makes sense, but I might not have thought that way until I took some more early childhood development courses and teaching courses. There's a lot of curriculum in grad school.

Kara considered children's role taking to be of particular interest and value. She saw the dramatic play to be a location for children to experiment and take on identities other than themselves. Additionally, she felt her place as a practitioner within that play was to observe, support, and provide the necessary questions and tools to move the play forward.

This was clear in the interactions I observed in Kara's classroom as well. While she did become immersed in the play of the children in the classroom, she remained Kara, the teacher—within the given play circumstances but in a supporting role. Kara's careful attention not only to her teaching goals but also to the play's purpose was evident in her facilitative choices and the way she assessed the play needs of her children in any given moment:

It's a way for the children to try on the roles. Where the teachers' role comes in is, how do I help them extend this? Mom or Dad goes to work. They use a phone. They drive a car. How do they get there? What do they actually do where they are, and what props can I bring to that? What language can I add to that? What books can I bring in to enhance those experiences?

In many of the play scenarios I observed, Kara "provided the glue" (Paley 1986, 123) for the children, tying together the dramatic threads that they had already established and connecting their play to her current curricular themes and teaching goals. While Kara held a "teaching" role when immersed in the play of her children, she often removed herself shortly after adding the "glue" to allow them space to play on their own.

Kara has seen changes in the way she, as a practitioner, has lost some of the opportunity to explore beyond the confines of the classroom with the children. She talked about the spontaneous adventures she used to have with her class in the surrounding areas of the school, looking for bugs around the shoreline of a pond or stumbling upon a construction site to observe. Kara talked about how challenging it can be to get the opportunity to explore outside the classroom because of the varied needs of the children. Because many children require in-classroom services throughout the day, she is often confined to the indoors. She shared, "It's wonderful that there are support services, but we can't just wander out . . . there are limitations. That's just . . . what it is. But it makes me sad. I've lost a little freedom as a teacher."

REFLECT

How do you like to "provide the glue" when you are engaged in the play of young children?

_____

_____

_____

_____

What role do you find yourself taking in and around children's play?

_____

_____

_____

_____

CHAPTER 7

The Maker

The child at play. *Sara/Indiana Jones is traveling through a system of tunnels in the basement. Her sisters are screaming with the excitement of the chase as they careen through the cardboard maze they have created out of leftover supplies from their mother's factory job. Sara quickly exits the boxes and grabs her flashlight, shining a beam of light through one of the many holes they have cut in the sides of the tunnel to create additional drama. "Agggghhhhh! Look out!" she yells, shaking the boxes and strobing the light by waggling the flashlight back and forth. The girls squeal and race toward the exit, hoping to make it out before something drastic happens. Sara clicks off the flashlight and the tunnel goes dark. "What's happening?" she whispers, "What's going to happen next?"*

ON AN ISLAND OFF THE southeast coast of the United States in 1987, Sara was born, joining her mother, father, and older sister. They lived there until Sara was four years old, when they decided to relocate and "start a new life," moving to a town on the outskirts of a small industrial city in the eastern United States. Here the family was joined by Sara's younger sister. Shortly after her sister's birth, Sara's parents split up and her father made his way back to the island from which they came. As a result of this upheaval, Sara's mother and girls moved to a neighboring town, and together they began to make a life for themselves in their new home. From the age of four until she was nine years old, Sara and her sisters lived with their mother in a townhome apartment complex outside of town with connecting yards in the back and a cul-de-sac for riding bikes in the front.

Sara's early play life existed in and around this home. She spent the majority of her playtime with her sisters and neighborhood kids, as well as the grandchildren of a nanny who would watch the girls while their mother was at work. Despite having a college degree from back home, Sara's mother (who was single during this early period in Sara's life) worked in a local factory to learn English and support the family, often working nights. The girls were not allowed to travel much beyond the house and the small yard, and so the majority of Sara's play memories from this time are inside. The house had two bedrooms upstairs, a living room and kitchen on the first floor, and a basement that held all of their toys, along with packaging materials leftover from their mother's work at the factory.

Sara and her older sister were close both in their friendship and their age. From first grade through high school, they were in the same class, participated in the same activities, shared a bedroom, and were, as she put it, "really, really close." Eventually their younger sister was old enough to join them in their play, ripe for "a little teasing and sibling rivalry." During this period of time, Sara remembers playing primarily indoors with her sisters.

The basement, where the Barbie Dreamhouse was located, was the locus of play for Sara and her sisters. Surrounded by concrete walls and all of their toys, Sara and her sisters would play for hours, creating adventure after adventure for themselves, using whatever they could get their hands on.

> We would play with boxes because it was very wide [in the basement]. So we'd just make like tunnels. . . . She [Mom] worked in a factory. Packaging, so maybe that's where she got them from. We would line up boxes, and they were tunnels, and then my sisters

would stand on the outside and go, "Okay, it's your turn to go to the sun." And then we'd go on the outside and shake it or poke holes in it and shine a light through it. We had to be resourceful.

Sara shared the excitement the girls experienced down in that basement, creating adventures for one another out of the things they found. This creativity continued in other areas of their play as well.

When the family eventually moved to a different neighborhood, their house had an entire floor just for the kids. The attic was a space the size of the footprint of the house, with enough room for serious play; it held all their toys, a television, and an arts and crafts table for making things. It was up in this space that Sara remembers a large amount of Barbie play taking place. The girls would spend copious amounts of time setting up the Dreamhouse furniture to get it just right before they could start playing out certain predetermined storylines with the dolls. Barbie went through a lot in that attic: cleaning the Dreamhouse with cotton swabs, dressing up in dresses and heels for parties, meeting boyfriends and having perpetual dramatic breakups, and going on wild adventures when invariably Barbie would end up hanging from a cliff about to drop to her doom. Ultimately, Barbie would get married, and the girls would prepare for the ceremony by creating wedding gowns out of toilet paper and tissue:

> Like toilet paper, or tissue paper. Put it on their heads and have,
> you know, a long veil. We wrapped them up because it was white,
> and we didn't really have white dresses. So we would just wrap
> them up and make their veils. It would be long, you know, like
> a little runner and stuff like that. I don't know where we got
> that from.

Thus, the Barbies would become brides with elaborate wedding gowns, outfitted for their big day, barring any unforeseen drama—which there usually was.

In their mother's room, the girls would create costumes out of the contents of her dresser. Ripping the sheets off the bed, the sisters created long gowns fit for princesses, adorned with old pieces of their mother's lingerie. Getting ready for the ball was often interrupted by some drama. "We'd always pretend to be princesses, and I was always the witch, or like the evil stepmother, and we'd be like, 'Lock them up in the tower.' Or, 'You can only escape if you solve these riddles.' Or like go [on] an adventure, get something and . . . bring it back." Sara remembered this type of dramatic play as "actually really fun" and related that she and her sisters found the joy of this play in the planning and the making, prior to the actual dramatization. The creativity involved in the stories she chose to share and her knack for extending play through her creations was apparent, and her ability to think creatively and playfully as an adult continues today.

REFLECT

What play materials were you drawn to in your childhood? What did you genuinely enjoy playing with?

The teacher at play. *Sara is up to her elbows in baking powder. She and two children are playing with the powder, which is meant to simulate clown face paint but has quickly turned into a sensory activity. Sara is repeatedly digging her hands into the tray of powder and letting it fall from her hands back into the tray. "It looks like it's snowing! It's snowing in here!" I am surprised at how it seems Sara is genuinely enjoying this activity. Her face contorts in such a way that only a sensory experience can achieve. "Oh, you know what would be cool? We have a sifter!" Sara jumps up and grabs a sifter from the cabinet. She shows the children how to use the sifter, modeling the action and grinning. The kids are getting the baking powder all over the floor. She sees a child notice this and reassures him, "We can vacuum later." Soon Sara has picked up the discarded sifter and continues to play. She makes it snow on her hands. "Oh, wow! That is so cool. Look at that!" she exclaims as she makes a mountain of baking powder on her hands. A child is standing on the periphery, and she calls him over. "Come stand over here with me," and she rolls up his sleeves. "Grab some of this. . . . Feel it. Did you try this?"*

Right out of high school, Sara knew she wanted to be a teacher. She was accepted into a teacher prep program at the state university near her home and immediately began working with children in a work-study program. Throughout her four years as an undergraduate, Sara worked with a variety of young children with a spectrum of educational needs, leading her to finish with a dual major in elementary education and special education. Soon after graduating, Sara began working as a learning support specialist in a charter school in her home state and spent her summers teaching in a migrant education program. She stayed in this position for two years, until she took a job as a dual language teacher in a fifth-grade classroom at a different charter school in the area. It was in the four years spent here that Sara gained considerable experience teaching older children social studies and science in Spanish in the school's immersion program. Eventually moved to pursue other interests, Sara left teaching to earn a master's degree in counseling and human services, with an interest in one-on-one community counseling and family therapy. Upon completing her master's degree, Sara began to look for work in a neighboring state, where she eventually found herself back in the early childhood classroom as a head teacher in the after-school program.

Throughout her schooling and her early teaching experiences, Sara thought of play as an important attribute in children's education, even if it was not at the forefront of her teacher education experience or the systems she taught in. Her preservice training encouraged teachers to create activities and learning experiences that were fun and engaging but not necessarily play based. Sara remembered taking specific classes that focused on kinesthetic learning and how to make things simultaneously fun and educational, but mainly she remembered a considerable amount of content-based teacher education. As Sara entered the workforce, she soon discovered the ways in which she could incorporate play into her own instruction with older children: tossing a ball to students who raised their hands to answer a question, creating games around reading material out loud, and making allowances for her students to engage with material in a playful way. "I always tried to make it—for me, I thought I was just like trying to get them engaged. But looking back, it was like a game and playing." In her early teaching life, Sara sought out hands-on activities, like leading the arts and crafts club, having her students create their own board games, and encouraging her older students to use PowerPoint and Prezi (presentation programs) to present the information they learned. It wasn't until Sara began working with young children and a play-centered curriculum that she discovered that play was so much more than simply making academic activities fun:

> At first it took me a lot to adjust to it. I feel like I always believed that play was important and fun for learning and engagement, but I never realized until [coming] here how important it was for building connections and relationships. . . . I look back at my fifth-grade teaching years, and I feel like I wasted a lot of time with curriculum and all of that. I feel like I look back now and it's just painful. Like, in a way, I didn't connect with them, and I could have.

Sara is often making things with and for young children. On multiple occasions, I watched Sara provide the children with an activity from materials she has made from scratch or crafting alongside them. During one particular week, the theme was the circus and Sara made a large circus tent from cut paper and placed it on the wall at child level. Next to the tent was glue and various bins of materials to place in the tent: puffballs, ribbons, foam peanuts, and animal stickers. Over and over, children were drawn to the area, drenching the tent with glue and adding texture to the picture they were creating together. As each of them came to work on the art project, Sara sat right there with them, narrating their choices and adding some items of her own. From my outsider perspective, she seemed to be genuinely enjoying herself, creating something new with the children.

REFLECT

How do you get your creative juices flowing?

What crafts do you enjoy creating alongside your children? Do you do any crafting on your own?

CHAPTER 8

Who I Am
Developing a Player Identity

AFTER I CONDUCTED the interviews with the four teachers, I began to look across their experiences—not at the individual per se, but at the collective experience of participating in this type of reflective practice that resulted in a rich, memory-based narrative. One of the most interesting things I found was that in the telling of their play story, each person experienced a similar type of identity shaping, or the building of a player identity. So what does this mean? Our identity is the lens through which we view ourselves in the world. It is the space we take up, our way of declaring ourselves on both a personal and a professional level. In telling our stories about play, we are participating in a deepening and a further shaping of our identity as players, and as teachers who play. This player identity is a key piece in the ways we understand our teaching; it is a large component to understanding **who I am** within the context of a play pedagogy.

Figure 1 (see p. 58) is a model that illustrates what happened to the teachers as they shared their play stories. The model represents the shared experience of participating in this type of reflection and shows how each of the participants evolved through the sharing of their play stories. I created this model to explore the commonalities found among the teachers' experiences of developing a play story. The model represents how through the development of a play history—from childhood play to adult play to teacher play—an identity begins to take shape, a definition of "Who am I as a player?"

REFLECT

As you look over the model, and the subsequent interpretation of its parts, think about how the writing prompts lead you to experience a similar type of identity shaping, a way of knowing about your personal relationship with play.

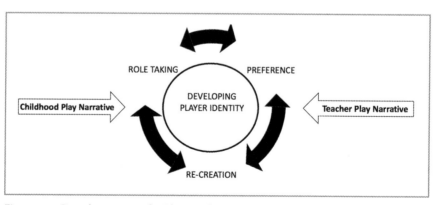

Figure 1—Development of a Player Identity

The arrows to the left and right represent the types of play narrative shared by each of the teachers I worked with: a childhood play narrative and a teacher play narrative. The center represents the experience in which each of the teachers began to develop a larger sense of selfhood around play. The model demonstrates (via the black arrows surrounding the circle) how each of the teachers at one point or another expressed **preference** and shared instances of **re-creation** and **role taking** throughout their stories of childhood play, as well as throughout their teacher play stories. These ways of thinking about play and play practice build on one another to strengthen a sense of ourselves as persons who play.

Preference

As the teachers shared their play stories, they evaluated particular kinds of play, establishing preferences for certain types of play over others. Taking preference into account draws our attention to the fascinating moments in which the four teachers revealed themselves as individuals with active interests in specific play activities both as children *and* as adults. In their rich descriptions of play that held and continued to hold their interest, the teachers began to merge the past and the present, a central process in building a player identity.

All of the teachers were very clear about what it was they liked to play as children. In the telling of their memories, each of the teachers exposed certain areas of their play world that they were drawn to: active play, doll-based dramatic play, quiet play, and so on. These preferences manifested simply, in the telling of what they did as children, and were reinforced via their expression of enjoyment and pleasure.

Each of the teachers carved out a play story for herself that only she could share—choosing the details that would illuminate the experiences that were most meaningful to her. Sara relished the description of the dollhouse she shared with her sister and the particularities of the play that made it so special: "We loved our dollhouse. It was pretty big. It was plastic. . . . The living room had all these little pieces, and the dining room had all these pieces, and you had to buy them separate, and then you could put them together. I loved setting up everything." By identifying what it was she loved about her dollhouse, she evoked her own enjoyment of that play, which came across in her storytelling. Her face brightened as she used her hands to accentuate her descriptions. The development of this narrative helped define how each individual liked to play and brought a sense of joy in recounting the unique circumstances that made a particular type of play special to her.

The teachers utilized memory and nostalgia in the shaping of themselves as players by describing what they liked to play and the reasons why they liked playing in that way. Megan's smile grew as she remembered a toy she loved: "Easy-Bake Oven! It was so fun because you cooked with a light bulb. You know, it's just weird, and it was just teeny-tiny little portions of fun things to eat. I'm sure it was absolutely awful, but it was so fun." Sharing moments when they identified the play materials they were drawn to as children deepened a connection to the play of their past, and perhaps more importantly, it exposed an affinity for specific types of play materials.

As the teachers shared the types of play and play materials they preferred to engage with and why they preferred them, they all pondered the attributes of that play. Kara talked about the outdoor play of her youth: "Well, my generation—we go out and play. With two big brothers and a little sister, you had your playmates right there. So that was nice. If it was cold, we would hike back in the woods, and we'd go skating on the ponds and think nothing of it." While Kara identified an activity she preferred, her clarification regarding what it was she loved about that play was accompanied by a larger defining statement about the way she played as a child. Her commentary exposes joyful pride in the way she played, as well as her assumption that children don't play that way any longer.

REFLECT

Finish this sentence: I loved playing _____ because
_____.

Conversely, the teachers were also able to identify the play activities they didn't care for. What they didn't like to play and why was typically connected to sibling conflict/relationships—the roughhousing of Kara's brothers, the bossy dramatic vision of Sara's sisters, and so forth—but interestingly, the conversation often shifted to broader statements about particular types of play or even shifted to the present tense. Megan shared her anxiety around the outdoor game capture the flag and other competitive sports like dodgeball: "I really don't like competitive stuff, and I don't like stuff that hurts; who wants to have a ball thrown at them? I don't find it fun at all." Taking a negative stance on a particular type of play is as much a part of shaping a person's player identity as positive statements about what they liked to play as children—both are formative aspects of one's preference.

REFLECT

Finish this sentence: I hated playing _____ because _____.

When the teachers talked about their childhood play, they took it upon themselves to self-name as a particular "type" of player, with some even making identity-shaping statements like "I was a Barbie girl" or "I was very tomboy" or "I was the little mayor." In taking stock of what it was they liked to play as children, they were creating space to identify themselves as a "type." For example, as a child I liked to muck about in the swamp near our house, mix potions in my mother's bathroom, and play with the discarded vegetables in the garden. I was a mess maker! These declarative statements were moments of self-definition and recognition, and they were woven throughout the teachers' storytelling. In the storytelling and shaping of their childhoods, the teachers declared and named an image of themselves as a player based on the preferences they discovered throughout the storytelling process.

REFLECT

Finish this sentence as it pertains to your childhood play: I was a _____.

This narrative, due to its focus on the past, involved a particular type of recall—one that involves the evocation not only of memories but also of the feelings and emotions tied into those memories. The identity of the player, shaped by the teachers and myself, was solidified in the collaborative titling of each of their play stories: Megan, The Puzzler; Jane, The Character; Kara, The Explorer; Sara, The Maker. In providing the rich details of what play activities they chose to participate in as children, they were carving a space to express the type of player they thought they were in childhood.

As they shared the history of play throughout their lifespan, the teachers' narratives often shifted to the ways in which these individuals played as adults. Far different from the play of their childhood or the play that occurred in the classroom, all of the teachers shared the playful ways in which they currently chose to spend their free time. Many of the teachers reinforced their enthusiasm for childhood preferences by providing examples of how they continue to play in this manner today. In describing what she loved about crafting, Sara, The Maker, talked about making event centerpieces by placing lights, beads, and flowers in glass jars, crystal vases, or spray-painted cigar boxes and adding flower arrangements. She talked extensively about the work that went into planning these centerpieces and the enjoyment she got out of that process:

> I guess the aesthetics of it. I like planning and thinking and piecing together: "Oh, this color looks good with this color with this scheme" or "This material I think will look good with this material." I start with the materials first and the color; then I think about the arrangement, the design, and then the structure. It's very relaxing to me.

Some of the teachers identified areas in which their childhood play has spilled over into how they choose to play as adults. Jane, The Character, laughed about how she had just recently gone to the Disney store and bought princess-themed Barbies because she simply couldn't help herself. Megan, The Puzzler, shared that she still likes to play word games and Scrabble with her family, much like she did with her grandparents as a child. In talking about their current play interests in conjunction with their discussion of childhood preferences, the teachers further aligned themselves as individuals who prefer to play in particular ways. Kara, The Explorer, related her childhood nature excursions to her current wanderlust. In talking about her summers up at the lake, she described how she continues to explore today. "I'll go on canoe trips too, sometimes by myself, where you port[age] the canoe, and then you stop at another island, and you sit and have lunch and read. What's better than that? Then you go for a swim. Oh, it's mental health. It's hard to come back here."

REFLECT

How do you currently spend your free time? What activities make you feel the most playful? Finish this sentence as it pertains to your adult play: I am a   .

When considered as something that occurs over the course of a lifetime, the development of a player identity includes the play of adults. In describing the attributes of their adult play, either as a continuance of their preferred childhood play activities or as a reinforcement of a love of a particular kind of play, the teachers shifted their discussion from something they *used* to love playing to something they *continue* to love playing. This merged the past and the present, adding further depth to the question "Who am I as a player?" and created a foundation from which to examine their teacher play in a more well-rounded way.

As the narrative shifted toward the role of these teachers within the play lives of their children, I asked them to describe what they preferred to play with in their classroom. This posed a challenge—teachers aren't typically asked what they truly enjoy doing over the course of their day, separate from the needs and interests of their children. Initially, many of the teachers had a hard time considering what they truly enjoyed doing, rather than discussing what the children in their classroom enjoyed. I pushed them to think specifically about activities and materials that excited them fully—calling on what they had shared about adult play as shown above: Kara's hiking, Sara's crafting, and so on. Drawing from the essence of that adult play, I asked them to tap into where in their daily working lives they feel moments of total involvement. That clarification allowed the teachers to think about and identify the ways in which they engage with play for purely personal reasons while in the classroom, and how these adult interests have connections to their childhood play.

Just as they had established preferences in their childhood play narrative, the teachers were able to define and emphasize the classroom play scenarios in which they were truly engaged in the act of play. Some were very explicit about which materials and activities they identified with the most. These types of declarative statements regarding what it is they genuinely appreciate about playing alongside children were a common response. Jane also used similar self-defining language as it pertains to play in the classroom, sharing, "I am a pretender. I do that always. . . . I think this is coming from me being an only child for most of my life, because I am a pretender. I mean, I *like* to do that." Here Jane not only claims to be a particular type of player but also draws a line between her play life as a child and her play life as an adult, further defining her player identity in a more complete way.

The teachers also shared areas of early childhood play that they don't care for as practitioners. All of the teachers were quick to address that while they knew the benefits of this particular type of play for children and willingly engaged with the children at play when needed, it was something they did not prefer to take part in. Megan recalled the play of her childhood as she discussed her general distaste for dramatic play:

> I absolutely hate it. I don't like pretending. I remember playing with my sister, and she would say, "You say this and then I say this and then I'll say this." So she was the director of this imaginative play. I would do it because it was just her and me, but as an adult, I do not like dramatic play. I never engaged in it with my own children. They have their own thing. They play lions and all sorts of games, but I never, ever got involved in it. And I cannot stand it.

Megan's vibrant description of her experience with dramatic play referenced her childhood experiences as an example of how her feelings about dramatic play originated and how these feelings manifested themselves in her adult life.

Sara, too, shared a dislike of the repetitive nature of dramatic play. While describing a play scenario with one child, she shared, "All he wanted to do was just go, 'Oh, help me, help me.' We were playing doll-houses and he just wanted to constantly go onto the top of the house and go, 'Help me, help me, help me.' There was no dialogue. I couldn't get anything going." By providing the details regarding what she disliked about this dramatic play (in this case, the repetitive nature of the play scenario), Sara further informed her growing definition of who she is as a player. Although she shared a love of setting up the furniture in her dollhouse as a child, she was not interested in the role playing in the dollhouse with that child. "I did like to play in my dollhouse, which was my favorite-est thing when I was younger, [but] I really did not enjoy playing [with] the dollhouse with him," she said. In stating what she didn't like about the repetition of certain types of play, she added more depth to her developing player identity.

Kara shared a perspective on the media-based play of her children that was in contrast with her childhood preference for outdoor play. In sharing her resistance to the superhero play in her classroom and the role of media in children's play lives, she stated, "We're bombarded with media. So much of it takes place the rest of the day, and I don't want to hear about some superhero 24/7." Kara's negative opinions about media-based play are meaningful, particularly when held in conjunction with her positive depictions of outdoor play. Her opinions about the play of some of the children, when held against her own experience, reflect a conscious personal evaluation and ranking of the two types of play.

These honest reflections about the unenjoyable aspects of playing with young children are a crucial piece in the formation of the preferences shared by the teachers. Statements like those mentioned previously highlight the possibility that each of these individuals comes into the classroom (as adult players but also as practitioners who play) with a particular set of interests and preferences that inform their engagement in children's play.

In telling their history with play and their subsequent reflection on classroom play, each of the teachers exposed preferences and opinions about the types of play they engaged in as children and later as adults. These evaluations lived within the rich descriptions of various play scenarios and play materials, as well as the strong assertions ("I loved" or "I hated") in regard to the types of play they experienced. The teachers shared similar evaluations as they took stock of what they enjoyed playing within the context of the classroom. In sharing what they liked to spend their time doing as children and what they are drawn to in the classroom as adults, the teachers began to give shape to two questions: "Who was I as a player?" and "Who am I as a player now?" In the investigation of these two questions, we discovered that the past and the present were not mutually exclusive and the merging of childhood play preferences and teacher play preferences was not uncommon. Some teachers made explicit connections between their childhood play and their teacher play, like Jane's statement about being an only child and her proclivity to pretend, or Megan's hatred of dramatic play throughout her lifetime. Others shared connections that were exposed through the interview process, like Kara's value placement on outdoor play and her reluctance to involve herself in the popular media in the play of her students, or Sara's love of setting up a dollhouse but her frustrations with the repetitive play of her student. Regardless, the preferences stated in the child play narrative and those mentioned in the teacher play narrative represent a context where the past informs the present, leading to a more comprehensive self-defined player identity. The development of these player identities (and all the reflection and evaluation it requires) helped reinforce a system of beliefs about play and its importance in the daily curriculum of young children. In addressing the questions, "Who was I as a player?" and "Who am I as a player now?" the teachers' attention naturally shifted to their play work and the role of these self-defined preferences in their teaching. After sharing their proclivities for play and further defining who they were as players, the teachers began to discover areas in which their interests and preferences merged with their teaching.

Re-creation

As the narrative shifted from the past to the present, it also turned the play story gaze from inward to outward, from the play preferences of the individual to the play interests of the children in their classrooms.

Re-creation involves the teachers' descriptions of participating in what they consider enjoyable play alongside their students, and the re-creation of play experiences for young children that match their own history and interests. Re-creation, as it pertains to reliving a childhood play experience within the context of the classroom or sharing similar experiences with children, brings feelings of pleasure, gratification, and satisfaction. When talking about their own play interests in relation to the play interests and needs of their students, the teachers uncovered a harmonious area where the two coexist and become a larger part of a player's identity—an individual who both plays and facilitates play. The teachers all shared areas of classroom play that they enjoyed experiencing alongside their students as well as on their own. While still seemingly connected to their personal preferences of certain types of play, the teacher play narratives shifted toward an examination of children's engagement rather than simply identifying what the teachers enjoyed doing. When sharing the positive experiences of playing alongside the students in their classrooms, the teachers expressed a level of satisfaction and pleasure in knowing that the children were experiencing a particular type of play. Kara shared, "Well, for me there's nothing more exciting than taking a walk in the woods, seeing and hearing the birds and the animals. That's part of the reason I like being here too, because it's their eyes and their enjoyment of nature all again." The voicing of this unique connection between the teachers' play interests and the engagement of the children marks an important location where the personal and professional aspects merge.

In exploring what play they genuinely enjoy working with and modeling alongside the children in their classroom, some teachers went so far as to reveal an impulse to re-create the play experiences of their youth. Jane shared, "I like them to be excited about different things. I remember how I played as a kid and what I liked to do, and I try to bring that back as much as possible." Memory and nostalgia are powerful here, as Jane unequivocally stated that she wants to "bring back" the play of her youth through the eyes of her students. Megan shared a similar sentiment:

> My physical play that was outside always had something to do
> with nature and animals, and really that's what I do with my kids

here at school. I bring in worms for them to play with; one of the students brought in a snake for them to see; we go on walks; and we follow the woodchucks. I mean, I love the science-y aspect of teaching children.

Examining her own history, Megan made explicit connections between her proclivities for certain types of play and her pedagogical actions that mirror her childhood experiences.

At a crucial pivotal point in every individual's play story, the narrative jumped to the present—from childhood and adulthood play habits to teacher play habits. The play story that began with narrative that expressed *who these women are as players* began to shift to narrative that expressed *who they are as teachers who play*. This turning point changed the focus from inward to outward and created space for redefining a player identity that encompassed both the personal and the professional.

REFLECT

What types of play are the most gratifying for you to observe or facilitate in your classroom? What are the most challenging?

_____

_____

_____

_____

Role Taking

When the teachers spoke about play personally (preference) as well as professionally (re-creation), they continued to give shape to their developing player identity. In talking about their own practice as teachers who play, the narrative also involved how they see themselves as facilitators of play. They did this in two ways: some directly related their role in the classroom to their personality and their developing player identity, while others took a more practice-based approach to their definition of their role within the play of their students.

In summarizing who they are within the context of their teaching, Jane and Sara framed their roles as facilitators as a personality trait. In other words, they associated their facilitations with who they are inherently as individuals. Jane shared, "I'm a silly person. I'm a funny, silly person. . . . And I really enjoy it, you know? I really do. I like getting silly. I like being funny with these guys and everything and go home when the day is done, but we all had a good day and it was really fun." Separate from any pedagogical strategy for facilitating play in her classroom, Jane shared her personal attributes that enhanced the play of her students. In taking up a facilitative role/playful identity in classroom play, Jane acknowledged her inherent value as a player within the context of the classroom. Sara also shared a more personal relationship with her role in the classroom, noting, "I feel like my role is to protect playtime. I want to make sure they play because, I don't know, it just goes by so fast. Even though you can grow up and play, but it's different." Though generalized, the roles defined by these practitioners represent an impactful set of skills in the classroom. Identifying their distinguished roles as facilitators of play further developed their player identity: as someone who is an important piece in the play lives of their students.

Teacher practice was a key piece for Kara and Megan as they began to identify their role within the context of facilitation. Kara shared, "My role is to help them communicate and work together, allow others in, and be a friend, share the kindness. . . . Well, I like to be the observer; to stop, look, and listen." The roles and attributes stated by Kara represent a defining of a particular area of professional engagement—one in which she as the teacher maintains an outside role to help the play along, as more of a guide than a player. This role taking aligns with the traditional framework interpreted by Elizabeth Jones and Gretchen Reynolds (2011). Similar to the roles defined in *The Play's the Thing: Teachers' Roles in Children's Play* (Jones and Reynolds 2011)—player, teller, mediator, scribe, communicator, stage manager, and planner— Kara illustrates the variety of hats she wears while engaging in children's play, like observer and communicator. Similarly, Megan shared, "My role—it varies depending on the day, depending on the child and the setting, but yeah, I am sometimes the facilitator, sometimes the parallel player." Here Megan also shared the various roles she takes up while also expressing her skill in assessing any ongoing play scenario to determine how she chooses to engage with children's play. The characterization of these roles is representative of a type of skill set related to teaching practice and play pedagogy, one that involves an in-the-moment judgment of the needs of the children at play and then acting accordingly. Rather than considering the role of the teacher as simply a reflection of their personality like Jane and Sara, Kara and Megan utilized what they know about children's play to define the attributes of their role.

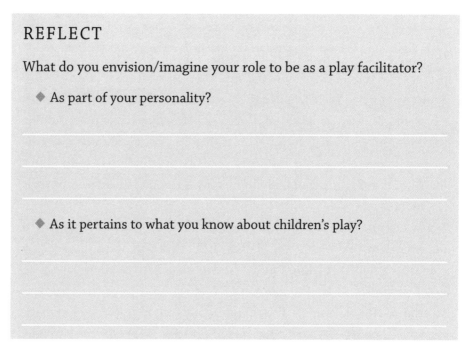

REFLECT

What do you envision/imagine your role to be as a play facilitator?

◆ As part of your personality?

◆ As it pertains to what you know about children's play?

When the teachers talked about the roles they take when facilitating play, they were able to move beyond simply telling me what they do and focus on what they do well. The foundation of our conversations provided a platform for examining and discussing where their skills reside in terms of play facilitation, deepening a sense of ownership and identity with teacher play.

In talking about play first through the lens of childhood and later practice, the teachers moved from sharing about memories of play toward active practice-based discussions about the play in their class-rooms. The merging of the past and present was a large part of every teacher's journey with the story-building process. This process—the exploration of a lifetime with play and the clarification of who one is as a player and who one is as a practitioner of play—was powerful, particularly when used together as a lens for examining practice.

REFLECT

Looking back on your writing prompts thus far, play around with giving your play story a title similar to those shared above (that is, The Maker, The Explorer, The Character, The Puzzler). You can pick more than one!

The _____

CHAPTER 9

What I Know
Intellectualizing Play

WHILE SHARING their play stories, the teachers seamlessly drifted into talk about play in a larger, more reflective sense. This included sharing thoughts and speculations about their theoretical understandings of play as well as looking more deeply at their own practice. It was as if the deepening of a player identity led the teachers to take a step back and look at their play history through a pedagogically based reflective lens. All at one point or another began to intellectually "play" with their pedagogy—both in a theoretical and a practical sense. When teachers began to discuss their own practice, they talked about play in three ways: **concepts of play**, **examination of play practice**, and **identifying locations for change**. This was a reframing and a defining of *what I know* within the context of a play pedagogy.

The following revised model, figure 2, (p. 74) shows the continuation of the play story process. The top portion of the model represents how the teachers engaged with their play stories as an identity builder, as seen in chapter 8. The lower part of the model represents a new location for thinking about play and play facilitation in a larger sense.

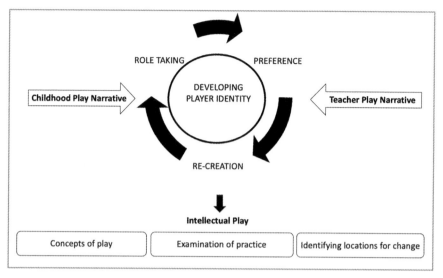

Figure 2—Intellectual Play

Concepts of Play

Discussing their professional identity, the teachers talked about play in a larger theoretical sense—play with a capital *P*. The teachers all shared different versions of what they think play means. This comes as no surprise, as a definition of play is infamously difficult to pin down, with myriad conceptions of the term in the multidisciplinary literature around play (Bergen 2014). The teachers were asked, "What is play?" throughout the research process, and their responses were as varied as their experiences.

When talking about definitions of play in the larger sense, some of the teachers theorized play through a personal lens. Sara shared, "When I think of play, I think of laughter. Where you're relaxed and not feeling like you're thinking about something else, you're enjoying what you're doing at that moment, and laughter comes to mind right away. So, if I'm laughing, then I'm playing around." In addition, some of the teachers developed concepts of play in contrast to their own personal, romantic recollections of play. Kara shared, "You had more empowerment, I think, too, to get out the good and the bad and the ugly. Now everything is so structured, and the whole term, the helicopter . . . the playdates. . . . I get nostalgic. Was it perfect? No. But would I like to start over again right now—no." In Kara's differentiation between her experiences and those of her students, she is conceptualizing and valuing play through the lens of her own childhood.

Discussing the attributes of play, much like defining it, is a complicated matter. Often the characteristics and attributes of play are a large part of what makes up its meaning. For example, Megan shared that play was "feeling joyful, exploring. Sometimes it involves touching, listening, looking; sharing with someone else; being silly sometimes." Different from the classifications of play found in the literature that attempt to codify and organize (see p. 11), the teachers simply expressed the observed actions and emotions that inform their larger theoretical understanding of play. Sara shared a similar sentiment, expressing thoughts about the place of play in young children's lives: "I feel like play is having fun, enjoying yourself, but then learning about yourself and learning about the people that you are playing with."

The teachers touched on the developmental discourse around play in various ways as well. Some of the teachers shared perspectives and definitions of play that were broad in nature. Jane shared, "Play is the center of all learning." Others were quick to make more detailed connections to the developmental impact of play. Sara stated, "I feel like through their playing they're exploring, and then they learn about things, or it triggers things that they've heard in the classroom . . . and maybe through play they can bring it back into the classroom." Through these discussions, the teachers deepened their conceptualizations of play within the context of young children's learning and development.

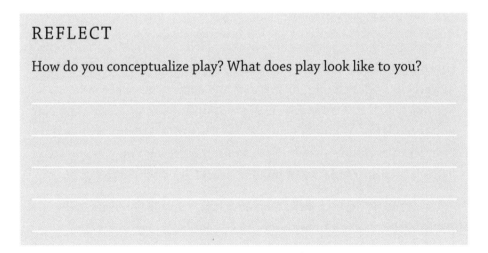

REFLECT

How do you conceptualize play? What does play look like to you?

Examination of Play Practice

When the teachers walked me through their different roles and perspectives in and around play, it made us reflect. In taking ownership over their role as a play facilitator, the teachers took stock of their daily practice for better or worse. For some, this reflection was evident in the teachers' positive acknowledgments of their current practice, while others identified areas for improvement. When highlighting the spaces and places in which they choose to enter the play of young children, or not, Sara shared:

> I feel like if I were letting them do it [play] on their own and me never engaging . . . that wouldn't be valuable. I do find more value in engaging with them and play, and I think that it's good. It's a good balance because in the morning, yeah, I don't play with them outside. Then in the afternoon, I do it. I'm really in.

Here, Sara described play facilitation within the framework of her history and her defined role in the classroom. Megan had a response based within a similar framework but with an opposite perspective on play facilitation:

> I realized when you were observing, that my style is not really to be "in there" with the kids, other than talking to them, and perhaps modeling the variety of ways to play with the materials. . . . In my mind, play with children is very dialogue based. Talking about what the child is doing, seeing, thinking . . . giving the child vocabulary, etc.

Accompanied by further conceptualizations of play, Megan acknowledged a particular style of play facilitation that she identifies with. In her previous statement, she clarifies the alignment of her beliefs and her practice, locating herself in a very specific position within the play of her students. While Megan and Sara identified distinctive ways to interact with children's play, Kara focused quite a bit on the fluidity of her role and the necessity of moving in and out of children's play:

> I love to be the next-door neighbor, jazz it up a little. Again, to be available, but not to be so immersed that I'm a play object—but

sometimes that does happen in the beginning. Then I do like to take a step back and see if they can figure out.

Kara highlighted how she reads a particular play situation and moves in and out of the play to accommodate the needs of the children. She was careful to explain that her role as a facilitator of play changes every day, from one activity to another, from child to child. Jane shared that her involvement in the play of the students is more personal:

> I feel like I have to [be engaged], you know, in order to get through the day and enjoy myself and know that the kids are going to go home with something substantial, you know? How much are you paying for this school? Come on.

Jane's interest in the play of the students in her classroom is heightened by her personal opinions about what her responsibilities are as an educator and to whom. In her mind, her active participation in the play of her students is important not only for her to get through the day but also to provide valuable play experiences for the families paying tuition for the school.

Each of the teachers shared a different perspective on the play needs of their students, and thus a different angle on play facilitation. These teacher/player identities vary but are all a strong component in developing a sense of self within a play pedagogy—a sense of self I watched each teacher develop throughout the storytelling process.

REFLECT

What are you proudest of in your play practice?

Identifying Locations for Change

Finally, teachers were quick to brainstorm together and individually to identify ways they could improve the current play practices in their classrooms. Each of the teachers noticed that the experience of sharing a play story had an impact on the way they view their own play practice, which was a catalyst for pedagogical change. Megan explained:

> Now I see how I have definitely passed down similar ideas of play to my own children and to my young students. And how some of my mother's attitudes about play were handed down to me. Your project has definitely sparked some introspection in me, and it has been an eye-opening process for me.

Here Megan clarified the ways in which the act of recalling past experiences with play led to introspection on her part. Examining her own play in tandem with the examination of her play as a teacher created a reflective space for Megan that introduced possibilities for pedagogical change. Later she continued, "I definitely see and feel a deficit in that dramatic play area. . . . So I think it's definitely going to make me think about how I plan activities and try to include the dramatic play area better." Her public examination and acknowledgment of herself as both a player and a teacher who plays (with all the evaluation it requires) strengthened an overall play ideology. Establishing this stance on play allowed her to wonder how she could improve her practice. Kara explicated this point: "Just by the very nature of doing this study with you, it made me think 'How can I play more, how can I stimulate more, what can I be doing, what am I forgetting, what am I missing?'" In viewing herself as an active participant in the play lives of children, Kara began to shift her gaze from a passive examination to an active one, geared toward pedagogical and facilitative change.

Sara and Jane also shared the impact of their experience within the research project. For them, the reflective process illuminated areas in their teaching that were more personal. Sara said, "Sometimes, like if I feel my mood is down, then I don't play as much with them. I feel like during this project it's made me so aware of that, like how a change in my mood is, like, 'Oh, she's not as interactive as she usually is.'" She also shared how the project has pushed that critical examination into active change, stating, "I feel like the project has helped me be more present in the moment." Jane, too, used the reflective process as a mode of introspection, realizing that her proclivities for playing had an impact. She discovered that in her time in the classroom, "I really do things I want to do," but when asked to look in an active way at her pedagogy, she reflected, "It can't be all about me all the time." Through this introspection, Jane sharpened her capacity to recognize both the strengths and weaknesses of her play ideology.

REFLECT

Are you starting to notice some areas in need of improvement in your play practice? What are they? What do you think you can do to change this?

When tasked with the work of building a play narrative from childhood to teacher-hood, each of the teachers ultimately formed a position on what they thought about play in a larger sense. Though teachers are often asked to give their opinions about various aspects of learning and development, be it in professional development, staff meetings, or with their peers, rarely do they consider these aspects within the context of themselves as players. Through the development of a play story, and the reflective process it required, each teacher examined their play pedagogy through a different set of eyes. These were the eyes of someone who has a history with, preferences in, and values surrounding play that are all their own. When pedagogy is considered fluid, developmental, and personal, this type of reflection becomes an opportunity for change. With their freshly defined player identity in the background, the teachers' theoretical understandings of play, the facilitative roles they identified, and the areas for improvement they noticed became more personal, meaningful investments in their pedagogical development.

In their descriptions of self as child and as teacher, all four teachers held fast to a very particular identity of a person who plays. In talking about these particular areas of their play lives and the ownership that comes along with identifying their strengths as a player, the teachers transitioned easily into discussions about teaching practice as it relates to play. In talking about their practice, the teachers naturally took a stance on play and play facilitation, creating a space to inhabit as a practitioner. This self-reflection was a bit more challenging, as it required the teachers to still consider themselves as a player, rather than digging into their thoughts and actions around how children experience play. Each teacher used their play trajectory as a springboard for regarding themselves as an adult player, evoking similar themes to those of their childhood play memories.

With this identity in tow, teachers began to examine their own practice through a new lens, examining larger theoretical understandings of play, as well as tackling a critical inventory of their own practice. This process of personal definition within the context of play asks teachers: Who was I? ➤ Who am I? ➤ What do I believe? ➤ What can I change?

REFLECT

Fill in this chart as it pertains to your play story:

◆ **Who was I?**

_____

_____

_____

◆ **Who am I?**

_____

_____

_____

◆ What do I believe?

◆ What can I change?

CHAPTER 10

Play Stories as Reflective Practice

PLAY STORIES PROVIDE an invigorating format for teacher reflection and self-assessment. This process presents an opportunity for teacher *reflection on past* (Clark 2019) that is geared toward awareness and pedagogical change. As described in chapters 8 and 9, creating a play story validates and reveals a player's identity, which can then be used to examine their practice. So what does that mean for us in practical terms? Let's consider this format of reflection in three productive ways: as an individual identity builder, as a pedagogical identity builder, and as a developer of personal practical knowledge. These formats for reflection are three dimensional, informing our identity as teachers and giving further shape to a holistic play pedagogy.

Play Story as an Individual Identity Builder

The narrative began by looking inward, focused on the traits of the individual. As the lifespan narrative shifted from childhood to adulthood, the gaze turned outward, to consider the roles that the individuals would take up within the context of the classroom. Personal identity and role taking are not isolated from each other in this process but rather informed by one another and the context in which they reside. If identity is to be considered fluid and ongoing (Beauchamp and Thomas 2009), it is the interplay between identity and role, past and present, that reshapes a newer, more complete, yet evolving player identity. From Jane's self-identification as a pretender and her establishment of such a role in the classroom to Kara's connection to the outdoors and her joy in discovering nature alongside her students, each individual shared two spheres of their play lives that inform one another, key pieces to understanding the play self in an authentic way. The identity of the teacher self and the roles taken up in the classroom inform and strengthen one another, creating an overarching player identity that encompasses a lifetime with play, both personally and professionally. The interrelatedness of personal and professional identity helps us understand the varied ways in which teachers may approach play, and examining this relationship can help deepen a sense of ownership of a play pedagogy.

Play Story as a Pedagogical Identity Builder

When play pedagogy is considered to be the merging of personal knowledge (**who I am**) and practice-based knowledge (**what I know**) (Clandinin 1985), it encompasses many aspects of the daily experience of play in the early childhood classroom. Teachers' choices around the materials, time, and formats for play are key decisions that are informed by a "pedagogical tool kit" that includes skills learned in teacher education programs as well as personal experiences, memories, and values.

By developing a player identity, the participants reframed their perspectives on themselves as practitioners, creating a platform for interpreting play academically. The four teachers reflected on larger conceptual ideas about play, examined their practice through the lens of their developing identity, and identified locations for pedagogical change.

In examining their theoretical understanding of play and what they considered to be their skills as players, the teachers took prideful ownership of the role they take up within the play of their students. Sharing the areas where they believe they playfully excel created space for a positive regard for their teaching and exposed the inherent play skills that each teacher possesses. After looking at what they do well, the teachers were also able to examine the areas where they may need a bit more attention. Each of the teachers located possibilities for change, highlighting the play they might be drawn to more often, areas they tend to avoid in the classroom, and what play activities could use more intentional facilitation. In examining their personal conceptualizations of play and current play practice through the lens of their player identity, teachers can have a clearer understanding of why they do what they do and take a comprehensive look at their pedagogical choices around play, pushing themselves to think about ways in which they can improve the quality of their play interactions in the classroom.

Play Story as a Developer of Personal Practical Knowledge

This process provided valuable input toward a newfound ownership and sense of pride over each individual's personal practical knowledge (Clandinin and Connelly 1988). This knowledge encompasses not only their play pedagogy but also their past experiences and identities with play. A play history and the teacher's reflection on it both became a part of the larger body of knowledge about play within the context of their teaching. The play history also spoke to their individuality as a practitioner who holds a set of values around play.

The acknowledgment and ownership of what these individuals believed about play and how they saw themselves as practitioners, together with a self-defined player identity, led them to think of their practice in a new way. Within this reflective process teachers carried their pasts into their present as a way to define themselves and their practice but also as a means of identifying areas for change. The culmination of the creation of a play history was a deepening of each individual's personal practical knowledge, or a teacher's body of knowledge that is informed by their lived experiences (Clandinin 1985).

In merging their perceptions of who they were as players with who they have become as practitioners of play, each of the participants expanded their body of knowledge toward a new way of knowing and looking at practice. This new way of viewing the play in their classrooms and their role in it strengthens a personal connection with play practice and further informs each individual's player identity. As shown in figure 3, this enhanced personal professional knowledge, resulting from this reflective work, feeds back into the evolving player identity of the practitioner. This way of knowing supports and informs further ownership and development of the identity of a player—in life and in practice.

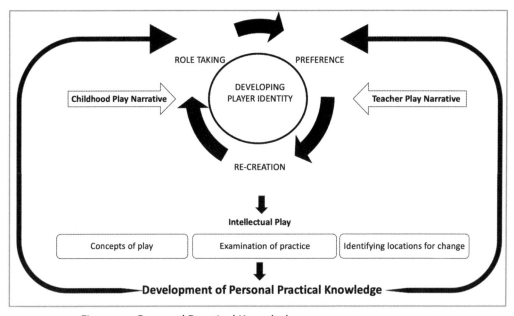

Figure 3—Personal Practical Knowledge

REFLECT

What would you consider to be the personal practical knowledge you carry with you into the classroom?

_____

_____

_____

CHAPTER 11

Disrupting
Play Stories

THROUGHOUT THIS BOOK I have shared the value of collecting play stories, developing a player identity, and using these stories to examine play pedagogy. Sharing our play stories opens us up to understanding the way we interact with play on a deeper, more personal level and leads to an understanding of our skills and weaknesses when we facilitate play. These facets of our player identity are part of the many ways we unconsciously engage with children's play in our classroom every day.

The development of a play story highlights the teacher's personal and professional ideas about what makes play valuable, raising the need for critical examination. In the critical work around children's play, multiple perspectives question whether adult intervention might prioritize certain modalities of play that may not align with the interests, needs, or cultures of the children we teach (MacNaughton 2009; Trawick-Smith and Dziurgot 2011). In other words, a teacher may carry with them a very particular idea of what play should look like that is specific to their singular experience rather than the experiences of the students in their classroom. Because of this, they may make play-based curricular choices that may not align with the experiences of the populations in which they teach. These choices include the materials they choose to use, the characters they inhabit, and the structure they implement in a classroom. For example, if a white middle-class teacher places a police uniform in the dramatic play area, they need to understand the different ways children may interpret this "character" and the ways they may enact some dramatic play scenarios. While the teacher may consider the police to be a representation of the community at large, many cultures may have a different perspective on the role of police in their everyday lives.

So how do we do better? We can start by recognizing how our cultural knowledge, familial background, and experiences with play are ever present in our teaching. This also shapes our perceptions of play and all the possible preconceived notions about play that come with our particular context. This awareness of our own context and positionality is important to bring into conversation with the understanding, established in the literature, that the meaningfulness of children's play is anchored in each individual child's experiences and context (Pacini-Ketchabaw 2014). In other words, just as the child's experience and sociological context is important in how we interpret their play, a teacher's experience and sociological context matters as well. Our capacity to interpret and facilitate play for all children suffers when teachers are unable to identify the personal and sociocultural biases that shape their interpretation of the play of young children.

When we create a play story, we are reinforcing our own play as valuable and impactful, but we must be cautious of making that the only way we think about our own play stories when we approach the actual play practices of children. This type of self-reflection also requires us to look critically at our practice and identify the areas in which a lifetime of play can create biases. In this chapter, we will explore ways to analyze our personal relationship with play. By holding our play experiences against those of our students, we can reach a deeper understanding of our biases and hold ourselves accountable for what we discover.

Making Assumptions about What Quality Play Looks Like

In our creation of our own play story, and the subsequent identity shaping that occurs through this process, we are developing a definition of what quality play looks like based on our personal experiences. However, in doing this, we may be in danger of unconsciously making assumptions about what we consider to be quality play experiences for *all children*.

During their interviews, all of the teachers painted the portrait of an idyllic setting, one in which children are playing with one another until dusk with no tension to be found within the play. This "polished" remembering of the past is not uncommon. This could be because of the pressure of working with a researcher and having these memories recorded, or it could simply be that when we look back on our childhoods we see them through idealized, rose-colored glasses (Harris 2017). Regardless, in sharing play stories we are exposing the areas in which we find the most nostalgia, pride, and ultimately value placement. The danger here is the possibility that one may prioritize a certain type of play over another, creating a personal hierarchy of play experiences. For example, as a teacher I value dramatic play. I grew up playing pretend a lot, and so that type of play has moved to the forefront of what I consider to be quality play for young children. Because of this, I carry some judgment around other types of play, and I value them less than dramatic play. In acknowledging this, I am furthering my awareness of the areas where I may be biased regarding what constitutes "good play." This awareness creates space for me to recognize these biases and to adjust my teaching accordingly.

While a personal perspective is a key piece in the development of a play pedagogy, it may not always be congruent with the play that occurs in our classrooms. Because of the multitude of ways in which young children play, it is important to recognize, identify, and examine the areas of play that do not align with our own ideas of what quality play looks like and to be open to other pathways for play. We can do this by honestly asking ourselves what we consider to be quality play experiences for children and then examining what we have left out—and why. We must carry with us an understanding that the play that holds meaning and value for us is an individual phenomenon, specific to a particular sociocultural context.

REFLECT

What are some assumptions you have made around what quality play looks like? What areas are left out?

_____

_____

_____

_____

Confronting Play That Makes Us Uncomfortable

After we engage with our history, and all the play preference that comes to light through that process, we can begin to revisit the types of play that we avoid in the classroom. Kara's acknowledgment that she doesn't care for superhero play and Megan's dislike of dramatic play are examples of how the sharing of a play story can expose the areas in which we are unskilled or unwilling as practitioners of play. We may be confused as to how to interact with certain types of play or simply feel a certain level of discomfort when it comes to play that doesn't fit our own experience.

Gun play, rough-and-tumble play, and superhero/good and bad guy play are all areas in which many teachers find themselves at an impasse: to allow for it or not? When observing these types of play, teachers are faced with a moment of self-assessment, one that involves taking stock of their comfort level allowing for and engaging with these types of play. In making these decisions, teachers may be unknowingly leaning on their own play experiences and what they consider to be "safe play" (Logue and Detour 2011). Play involving guns, roughhousing, or superheroes may live outside our personal frame of reference, and so we may be quick to put an end to what could very well be valuable play. When witnessing these types of play, we must ask ourselves, "What is it about this play that is making me uncomfortable?" and "Could I possibly allow space for these types of play and sit with my discomfort?"

Teachers are faced with a judgment call when interacting with play that could be considered "rough," and often their frame of reference for these judgment calls is how they grew up playing themselves. One teacher may consider the rough play of young children to be completely safe, if not a healthy part of their growth and development. Another teacher may see a scraped knee as going a bit too far and put a stop to any rough play they encounter. With physical and emotional safety as the main goal, teachers have to exist in this space that has quite a bit of "wiggle room" and often is informed by our personal connections to and experiences with these types of play.

When witnessing play that makes us uncomfortable or play that we are quick to put a stop to, we also must acknowledge that some types of play may read differently on different bodies. Counter to the experiences of a primarily white and female early childhood workforce (IOM and NRC 2012), the play of boys, particularly Black boys, is often considered "unsafe" or "dangerous." This often leads to disproportionate discipline and ultimately the elimination of certain types of play on the playground and in the classroom (Bryan 2020; Ladson-Billings 2011; Wright 2019). This reminds us that there are long-term material consequences to how teachers evaluate the play of children of color, which is why this critical aspect of play story work matters. In exploring our history with play, we must confront our positionality and our role in the systemic racism that inhabits the spaces in which we teach. By examining our play stories, we uncover and question our discomforts more deeply. Acknowledging a particular way of knowing about play helps us to unpack why we find certain types of play to be disquieting. Ask yourself this: **When and where** do I put a stop to children's play? **Who** is doing the playing that I find problematic? Do these types of play run counter to your own play story? If so, you must acknowledge your implicit bias and take ownership of the possibility that you are controlling children's play for the wrong reasons.

REFLECT

What is a type of play that makes you uncomfortable? Why does this particular type of play make you uncomfortable? What are the qualities of this play that you find problematic? What are the reasons for this? What can you do to engage in this play more productively?

Play Pedagogy as Positionality

Our play history is, in essence, a sociocultural lens through which we view the play of the children in our classrooms. We interact with play from a unique perspective, based on our experiences and expectations of what play is and looks like. Play stories are helpful in understanding our play pedagogy in a deeper way, but at the same time, they need to be a reminder that not all experiences look the same. Evaluations we make of play in real time do not occur in a vacuum. Our sociological context informs how we perceive the play of children. For this reason, when we facilitate the play of children who hold a positionality different than our own, we need to account for the implicit bias in our own play story. We do this by acknowledging the specific sociocultural identity that we carry with us every day, or our positionality. For example, as a white, able-bodied, middle-class woman who grew up in a rural geographic location, I have a very specific body of knowledge that is informed by my history and experiences with that particular privileged identity. This identity is the lens through which I view the play of young children, for better or worse. The **who I am** of my play pedagogy is highlighted as a space for critical examination and adjustment when it comes to the play of all young children. When ascertaining our play positionality we ask, "What identities do I inhabit (race, class, gender, ability, and geographic location) and how is this identity significant to the way I view and facilitate play?"

REFLECT

How could the biases of a white teacher influence the way the teacher regulates the play of children of color?

How could the assumptions of an able-bodied teacher influence the teacher's assessments of what kinds of play are safe or appropriate for children with disabilities?

How does a middle-class teacher interpret the play of children living in poverty?

When we interact with our play history, we need to take stock of the ways in which we may be biased regarding play and open ourselves up to understanding its cross-cultural multitudes. It does not always look the way we experienced it, nor is it always reflected in the white, middle-class framework of what is considered to be developmentally appropriate play (Bryan 2020; Souto-Manning and Rabadi-Raol 2018). When we as a field consider what we mean by "best practices" around play, it begs the question, "Whose practices?" Quality play can take many forms, and it does not always fit the ways in which early childhood professionals are taught and expected to interpret play.

With introspection comes the responsibility to shift our gaze outward. After we have uncovered our own play stories, we must then remove ourselves from the center of a play pedagogy and turn toward the play lives of our students. In doing this, we are inhabiting a more holistic, three-dimensional conception of what play looks like and creating space for both self-understanding and social awareness. This is a location in which the **who I am** and **what I know** intersects with **who I teach**.

I believe that it is our responsibility as practitioners to further our critical understanding of ourselves and to think of our player identity as a component of our positionality. Our race, class, gender, and ability are key parts of ourselves, and our play stories are formed, in part, by those aspects of our identity. The hope is that a reflective process such as this creates space for us to reflect on our past in such a way that it enhances an awareness of a possible imbalance in play pedagogy. Space in the play story model, figure 4, is necessary to disrupt the development of teachers' personal practical knowledge, allowing for critical examination. This is a place in the reflective process in which we must stop and examine how our identity as a player could be a bias when interpreting the play of young children. After going through the experience of play story creation and all the reflection and reacquaintance with pedagogy it requires, teachers must hold their ever-shifting player

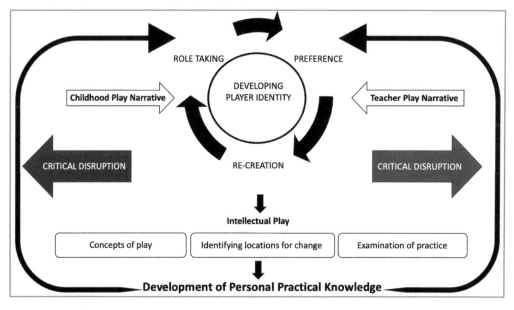

Figure 4—Disrupting Play Stories

identity and play pedagogy against self-evaluation. In asking, "What can I change?" teachers are able to engage with their personal practical knowledge, evaluate it critically, and examine their play pedagogy as **play positionality**.

REFLECT

What is your play positionality?

_____

_____

_____

What are some possible biases you may have when interpreting the play of children who have a different positionality than you?

_____

_____

_____

Holding a critical reflective process allows teachers to examine themselves and their actions and to make very real, significant change. The hope is that teachers' critical self-awareness of their play story, and how that play story influences their choices and evaluations as classroom play facilitators, can have real material positive consequences for the children they have contact with. In doing this we are opening ourselves to

◆ forms of play we would otherwise not engage with;

◆ forms of play that are unfamiliar to us;

◆ flexibility in our evaluations of play as "high quality" or "safe"; and

◆ last but not least, expanded capacity to notice and self-correct social prejudices that impact our evaluations of the play of marginalized children.

CHAPTER 12

Practice

SO WHAT DOES THIS MEAN in everyday teaching practice? In sharing our experiences with play in and out of the classroom, we expose our strengths as players and as practitioners who play. When we collect our impressions of who we were as players and identify ourselves as a person with a particular set of play skills, we deepen our sense of belonging surrounding play and expand our knowledge around the act of play. We develop a sense of ownership of our playful selves and take pride in the work we do playfully with the children in our classrooms. We find ourselves more fully actualized practitioners with a richer understanding of how we view and participate in the play of young children. Acknowledgment and ownership of our play story can reframe our identity, fostering a productive form of self-assessment that would be useful in many formats.

Through this reflective practice we can

- identify the types of play we like and are comfortable facilitating in our classrooms and lean into them;
- identify things we dislike or are uncomfortable with and find ways to approach those play situations with self-awareness; and
- identify ways we can build our pedagogical repertoire.

Play stories can push us to consider ourselves beyond classroom life and open up the possibility of understanding that practice is personal. In doing this type of reflective practice, we consider our teaching as a fluid experience, informed by our past and our present, in and out of school contexts. It is a form of teacher reflection that rejects the identity and role of the teacher as simply a vessel for curriculum implementation and exposes the human experience as a large piece in the shaping of a teacher identity. Play stories also provide a counternarrative to the dominant discourse in early childhood education by shifting the perspective to the voices of teachers, an area lacking in our field (Ryan and Goffin 2008). In asking who early childhood teachers are and what drives the decisions they make, we pay attention to the lives of those in the classroom and elevate the voices of teachers.

The collection and sharing of play stories has value in multiple settings. Both preservice and practicing teachers benefit from this type of multidimensional reflective practice, to come out of a play story experience with a more well-rounded understanding of the ways in which they engage with play.

Preservice Teachers

In teacher preparation programs, courses designed around play-based curriculum would benefit from including this reflective practice. Preservice teachers can use the collection of play story interviews and personal narrative building as a vehicle for understanding their own ideas about play as well as the ideas and experiences of their peers. Asking students to formulate and conduct play story interviews with one another allows them to examine play from another perspective while deeply examining their own experiences with play. This, in turn, informs their practices and conceptions about teaching. Taking a deep dive into the play narrative of their peers, listening or reading transcripts of themselves, and re-storying their own play narrative gives students a chance to reexamine play as not just a frivolous activity for children but a large piece of who they are, as humans and as future teachers. Additionally, by exploring who they wish to become as teachers through the analytical lens of who they were as children, teacher education students can gain a deeper understanding of their play skills and understand their own place in the early childhood classroom.

Practicing Teachers

Practicing teachers can use play history narrative for professional development or for supervision purposes. Professional development is typically focused on classroom activity and confined to one session with little to no follow-up. Using this format of reflection and self-assessment can be cooperative and ongoing. Possible professional development could involve play memory journaling or interviews and group discussions to engage in the process with peers. Asking teachers to participate in and collect play history interviews with one another creates space to engage with each other playfully and personally while examining practice in a more holistic way. If teachers engage in play history interviews as a form of professional development, the activity becomes personal, reflective, and conversational.

Every day in every classroom, teachers walk in the door with at least two things: a history and a personal pedagogy. This work examines the possibility that history and pedagogy do not live separately but rather inform one another. When teachers are viewed as dynamic individuals with varied sources of contextual influence on pedagogy (Rimm-Kaufman et al. 2006), the personal and the professional are inextricable.

The gatekeepers of play are teachers, the ones who are in the classroom every day making pedagogical choices that incorporate or exclude play for the children in their classrooms. Providing a platform for teachers to understand their play pedagogy from a more holistic perspective and to self-identify where they really playfully shine in their classrooms creates space for teachers to think of themselves as skilled players—a play asset to the classroom, and thus more invested in the play of young children.

Appendix
Play Story Interviews

OVER THE COURSE of this book, you have had the opportunity to self-reflect in writing along the way. Those writing prompts were meant to keep you thinking about your own play story as you read and to connect more deeply to the content of the book. Here you will find two play story interview protocols meant to be conducted with a partner and shared aloud. One protocol is for practicing teachers and one is for preservice teachers who may or may not have had some classroom experiences.

These interviews are most effective when they are conducted in pairs so you have the opportunity to free-associate and dig into your memories of play. If you have explored this book as part of professional development, if you are in a class that is using this book as a text, or if you are reading this on your own, find a partner, coworker, or anyone willing, and begin unpacking your own play story. You may find it helpful to record your story so you can listen later, but the goal of this interview is to reflect out loud and look at your practice through the lens of your own experiences.

Practicing Teachers

Family

Tell me about the members of your family, starting with your parents/caregivers.

Did you have siblings? If so, did you play with them? What would you play?

Were your parents/caregivers playful? How did they engage with play?

How would you describe your childhood play? Can you give some examples?

Spaces and Materials

You spent a lot of your childhood in (location). Can you describe the area to me?

What were the spaces in the surrounding area and your home that stick out the most to you?

Can you walk me through your childhood home? What would you be doing in those spaces?

How did children in your area spend their time? Why do you think they were drawn to that?

What childhood toys/materials do you remember playing with in these spaces?

School

Where did you go to school? What do you remember about your early experiences in school? What were you drawn to? What didn't interest you?

Walk me through an after-school afternoon when you were young.

Adult Play

How do you spend your downtime now?

Do you consider yourself playful? How so?

How would you define the word *play*?

Teacher History

How did you end up here at this school?

What do you remember about the topic of play in your teacher preparation program?

How do you see play as it pertains to children's lives and children's education?

Classroom

If I asked the children to describe how you play with them, what would they say?

How do you see your role in relation to that play? Could you give me some examples?

How do the children in your classroom like to play?

What do you genuinely like to play with in the classroom?

What do you like to do when children are playing?

Preservice Teachers

Family

Tell me about the members of your family, starting with your parents/caregivers.

Did you have siblings? If so, did you play with them? What would you play?

Were your parents/caregivers playful? How did they engage with play?

How would you describe your childhood play? Can you give some examples?

Spaces and Materials

You spent a lot of your childhood in (location). Can you describe the area to me?

What were the spaces in the surrounding area and your home that stick out the most to you?

Can you walk me through your childhood home? What would you be doing in those spaces?

How did children in your area spend their time? Why do you think they were drawn to that?

What childhood toys/materials do you remember playing with in these spaces?

School

Where did you go to school? What do you remember about your early experiences in school? What were you drawn to? What didn't interest you?

Walk me through an after-school afternoon when you were young.

Adult Play

How do you spend your downtime now?

Do you consider yourself playful? How so?

How would you define the word *play*?

Teacher History

How did you end up in a teacher education program?

What have you learned about the value of play in your current teacher preparation program?

How do you see play as it pertains to children's lives and children's education?

In the Field

(Answer the questions below based on your experiences thus far in the classroom.)

If I asked some of the children you have worked with to describe how you play with them, what would they say?

How do you see your role in relation to that play? Could you give me some examples?

How have you noticed the students in your classroom like to play?

What do you genuinely like to play with in the classroom?

What do you like to do when children are playing?

References

Bauml, Michelle. 2011. "'We Learned All about That in College': The Role of Teacher Preparation in Novice Kindergarten/Primary Teachers' Practice." *Journal of Early Childhood Teacher Education* 32 (3): 225–39.

Beauchamp, Gary, and Linda Thomas. 2009. "Understanding Teacher Identity: An Overview of Issues in the Literature and Implications for Teacher Education." *Cambridge Journal of Education* (39) 2:175–89.

Bergen, Doris. 2014. "Foundations of Play Theory." In *The SAGE Handbook of Play and Learning in Early Childhood*, edited by Liz Booker, Mindy Blaise, and Susan Edwards, 9–21. Thousand Oaks, CA: SAGE.

Bodrova, Elena, and Deborah J. Leong. 2024. *Tools of the Mind: The Vygotskian Approach to Early Childhood Education*. 3rd ed. Upper Saddle River, NJ: Prentice Hall.

Bryan, Nathaniel. 2020. "Shaking the *Bad Boys*: Troubling the Criminalization of Black Boys' Childhood Play, Hegemonic White Masculinity and Femininity, and the *School Playground-to-Prison Pipeline*." *Race Ethnicity and Education* 23 (5): 673–92.

Clandinin, D. Jean. 1985. "Personal Practical Knowledge: A Study of Teachers' Classroom Images." *Curriculum Inquiry* 15 (4): 361–85.

Clandinin, D. Jean, and F. Michael Connelly. 1988. "Studying Teachers' Knowledge of Classrooms: Collaborative Research, Ethics, and the Negotiation of Narrative." *Journal of Educational Thought* 22, no. 2A (October): 269–82.

Clark, Katelyn. 2019. "Play Then and Now: A Narrative Study of Early Childhood Teachers' Play Histories and Practices." PhD diss., Rutgers University. ProQuest (13810478).

Cook, Deirdre. 2000. "Voice Practice: Social and Mathematical Talk in Imaginative Play." *Early Child Development and Care* 162 (1): 51–63.

Copple, Carol, and Sue Bredekamp. 1986. *Developmentally Appropriate Practice*. 1st ed. Washington, DC: NAEYC.

Dewey, John. 1910. *How We Think*. Boston: Dover.

———. 1916. *Democracy and Education*. New York: Macmillan.

———. 1933. *How We Think: A Restatement of the Relation of Reflective Thinking to the Educative Process*. Boston: D.C. Heath & Co.

Erikson, Erik H. 1963. *Childhood and Society*. 2nd ed. New York: Norton.

Freud, Sigmund. 1956. *Delusion and Dream*. Boston: Beacon Press.

Gmitrová, Vlasta, and Juraj Gmitrov. 2003. "The Impact of Teacher-Directed and Child-Directed Pretend Play on Cognitive Competence in Kindergarten Children." *Early Childhood Education Journal* 30 (4): 241–46.

Harris, Paula. 2017. "Nostalgia and Play." In *Practice-Based Research in Children's Play*, edited by Wendy Russell, Stuart Lester, and Hilary Smith, 19–33. Bristol, UK: Policy Press.

Hirsh-Pasek, Kathy, Roberta Michnick Golinkoff, Laura E. Berk, and Dorothy G. Singer. 2009. *A Mandate for Playful Learning in Preschool: Presenting the Evidence*. New York: Oxford University Press.

IOM (Institute of Medicine) and NRC (National Research Council). 2012. *The Early Childhood Care and Education Workforce: Challenges and Opportunities: A Workshop Report*. Washington, DC: National Academies Press.

Johnson, Colleen. 2002. "Drama and Metacognition." *Early Child Development and Care* 172 (6): 595–602.

Jones, Elizabeth, and Gretchen Reynolds. 2011. *The Play's the Thing: Teachers' Roles in Children's Play*. 2nd ed. New York: Teachers College Press.

Ladson-Billings, Gloria. 2011. "Boyz to Men? Teaching to Restore Black Boys' Childhood." *Race Ethnicity and Education* 14 (1): 7–15.

Logue, Mary E., and Ashlee Detour. 2011. "You Be the Bad Guy: A New Role for Teachers in Supporting Children's Dramatic Play." *Early Childhood Research and Practice* 13 (1). https://files.eric.ed.gov/fulltext/EJ931230.pdf.

Logue, Mary E., and Hattie Harvey. 2010. "Preschool Teachers' Views of Active Play." *Journal of Research in Childhood Education* 24 (1): 32–49.

MacNaughton, Glenda. 2009. "Exploring Critical Constructivist Perspectives on Children's Learning." In *Early Childhood Education: Society and Culture*, edited by Angela Anning, Joy Cullen, and Marilyn Fleer, 43–54. London: SAGE.

Marbach, Ellen S., and Thomas D. Yawkey. 1980. "The Effect of Imaginative Play Actions on Language Development in Five-Year-Old Children." *Psychology in the Schools* 17 (2): 257–63.

Meyers, Adena B., and Laura E. Berk. 2014. "Make-Believe Play and Self-Regulation." In *The SAGE Handbook of Play and Learning in Early Childhood*, edited by Liz Brooker, Mindy Blaise, and Susan Edwards, 43–55. Thousand Oaks, CA: SAGE.

Miller, Edward, and Joan Almon. 2009. *Crisis in the Kindergarten: Why Children Need to Play in School*. College Park, MD: Alliance for Childhood.

NAEYC (National Association for the Education of Young Children). 2022. *Developmentally Appropriate Practice in Early Childhood Programs: Serving Children from Birth through Age 8*. 4th ed. Washington, DC: NAEYC.

Neuman, Susan B., Carol Copple, and Sue Bredekamp. 2000. *Learning to Read and Write: Developmentally Appropriate Practices for Young Children*. 1st ed. Washington, DC: NAEYC.

No Child Left Behind Act of 2001, 20 U.S.C. www.congress.gov/bill/107th -congress/house-bill/1.

Pacini-Ketchabaw, Veronica. 2014. "Postcolonial and Anti-racist Approaches to Understanding Play." In *The SAGE Handbook of Play and Learning in Early Childhood*, edited by Liz Brooker, Mindy Blaise, and Susan Edwards, 204–15. Thousand Oaks, CA: SAGE.

Paley, Vivian. 1986. "On Listening to What the Children Say." *Harvard Educational Review* 56 (2): 122–32.

Pestalozzi, Johann H. 1894. *How Gertrude Teaches Her Children*. London: Routledge & Kegan Paul.

Piaget, Jean. 1962. *Play, Dreams and Imitation in Childhood*. New York: Norton.

Pinar, William F. 1981. "'Whole, Bright, Deep with Understanding': Issues in Qualitative Research and Autobiographical Method." *Journal of Curriculum Studies* 13 (3): 173–88.

Podlozny, Ann. 2000. "Strengthening Verbal Skills through the Use of Classroom Drama: A Clear Link." *Journal of Aesthetic Education* 34 (3–4): 239.

Rimm-Kaufman, Sara E., Melissa D. Storm, Brook E. Sawyer, Robert C. Pianta, and Karen M. LeParo. 2006. "The Teacher Belief Q-Sort: A Measure of Teachers' Priorities in Relation to Disciplinary Practices, Teaching Practices, and Beliefs about Children." *Journal of School Psychology* 44 (2): 141–65.

Roopnarine, Jaipaul, and James E. Johnson, eds. 2012. *Approaches to Early Childhood Education*. 6th ed. Upper Saddle River, NJ: Prentice Hall.

Roskos, Kathleen A., and James F. Christie, eds. 2007. *Play and Literacy in Early Childhood: Research from Multiple Perspectives*. 2nd ed. Mahwah, NJ: Lawrence Erlbaum Associates.

Rousseau, Jean Jacques. (1762) 1911. *Émile, or On Education*. New York: E.P. Dutton.

Ryan, Sharon, and Stacie G. Goffin. 2008. "Missing in Action: Teaching in Early Care and Education." *Early Education & Development* 19 (3): 385–95.

Ryan, Sharon, and Kaitlin Northey-Berg. 2014. "Professional Preparation for a Pedagogy of Play." In *The SAGE Handbook of Play and Learning in Early Childhood*, edited by Liz Brooker, Mindy Blaise, and Susan Edwards, 204–15. Thousand Oaks, CA: SAGE.

Schön, Donald A. 1983. *The Reflective Practitioner: How Professionals Think in Action*. New York: Basic Books.

Smilansky, Sara. 1968. *The Effects of Sociodramatic Play on Disadvantaged Preschool Children*. New York: John Wiley and Sons.

Souto-Manning, Mariana, and Ayesah Rabadi-Raol. 2018. "(Re)Centering Quality in Early Childhood Education: Toward Intersectional Justice for Minoritized Children." *Review of Research in Education* 42 (1): 203–25.

Sutton-Smith, Brian. 1997. *The Ambiguity of Play*. Cambridge, MA: Harvard University Press.

Trawick-Smith, Jeffrey, and Traci Dziurgot. 2011. "'Good-Fit' Teacher–Child Play Interactions and the Subsequent Autonomous Play of Preschool Children." *Early Childhood Research Quarterly* 26 (1): 110–23.

US Department of Education. 2009. *Race to the Top Program Executive Summary*. Washington, DC: US Department of Education. www2.ed.gov /programs/racetothetop/executive-summary.pdf.

Vygotsky, Lev S. 1978. *Mind in Society: The Development of Higher Psychological Processes*. Cambridge, MA: Harvard University Press.

Wright, Brian. 2019. "Black Boys Matter: Cultivating Their Identity, Agency, and Voice." *Teaching Young Children* 12 (3): 4–7.

Index

academics, studies on play as important to, 8
adult play
childhood play as informing, 66
as choice, 18
as continuation of childhood play,
62
disliked, 92
as part of play identity, 63
reflecting on, 63

Barbie dolls and Dreamhouse, 50, 51,
59–60
Bodrova, Elena, 11
Bredekamp, Sue, 10

cognitive development
dramatic play and, 8
play and
Piaget and, 9
Vygotsky and, 10
constructivism, 8
Copple, Carol, 10
crafts and crafting
reflecting on, 55
in Sara's story, 62
creativity
in dramatic play in Sara's story,
51–52
reflecting on developing, 55
curriculum, based on dramatic play, 11

Developmentally Appropriate Practice
(Copple and Bredekamp), 10
Developmentally Appropriate Practice
(NAEYC), 11–12
Dewey, John, 9

dolls and dollhouses
in Jane's story
as adult, 36, 62
love of, as child, 35
in Megan's story, 25, 26
in Sara's story, 50, 51–52, 59–60
dramatic play
cognitive development and, 8
curriculum based on, 11
experimentation and new identities
in, 46
in Jane's love of
as child, 33, 35–37
as teacher, 38, 39
Kara as teacher and, 45
knowledge building and, 11
materials for, 49, 50–52
media format and, 35–36
Megan's dislike of, 26–27, 30–31, 64
roles children take on in, 45–46
in Sara's story
adventurous, 49, 50–52
creativity and, 51–52
dislike of repetitive nature of, 65
dolls and dollhouses and, 50,
51–52, 59–60
See also dolls and dollhouses

Émile, or On Education (Rousseau), 9
emotions, evocation of, 62
Erikson, Erik, 9–10

feelings, evocation of, 62
Freud, Sigmund, 9–10

instruction and child's zone of proximal development, 11

self-regulation and development of
    play, 10
The Sims "virtual dollhouse" world,
    36
social emotional development and
    play, 9–10
sociocultural contexts of play
    learning and, 10
    play pedagogy and, 92–93
    as reflection of, 18
Sutton-Smith, Brian, 15
symbolic thinking and development
    of play, 10

teachers
    benefits of play stories for, 99
    commonalities among experiences
        of, developing player identity,
        57–59
    play stories interview prompts for,
        101–103
    re-creation by, 58–59, 66–68
    reflecting on role in play of, 13, 17,
        40, 68
        own role, 47
        providing "glue," 47
        role as facilitator, 70
    role in play of

as changing as needed, 69–70,
    76–77
as facilitator, 8, 28–29, 30, 69, 76
as insider facilitator intentionally
    and dynamically intervening,
    11–12
interplay with own player
    identity, 84
memories and, 67–68
as observer creating environment,
    9, 46, 76
as outside observers, 10, 12
player identity and, 66–68
play preferences and, 63–64,
    65–66
as protectors, 69
re-creation and, 66–68
Vygotskian-based curriculum
    developers and, 11
Teachers' Roles in Children's Play (Jones
    and Reynolds), 69
Tools of the Mind (Bodrova and
    Leong), 11

Vygotsky, Lev, 10–11

zone of proximal development (ZPD),
    10–11